The Economy to Come

IN PROPHETIC CONTEXT

What will happen when your money fails?

WILLIAM R. GOETZ

HORIZON BOOKS

A DIVISION OF CHRISTIAN PUBLICATIONS, INC.
CAMP HILL, PENNSYLVANIA

Horizon Books
a division of Christian Publications
3825 Hartzdale Drive
Camp Hill, PA 17011
www.cpi-horizon.com

ISBN: 0-88965-175-2

98 99 00 01 02   5 4 3 2 1

A NOTE FROM THE PUBLISHER

The Economy to Come offers only general observations gleaned from the author's research and, particularly in regard to Y2K suggestions, makes no specific recommendations.

The book is based on information believed to be reliable, and every effort has been made to make *The Economy to Come* as complete and accurate as possible utilizing the information available as of the date of printing, but its accuracy and completeness cannot be guaranteed.

The reader should use the book only as a general guide to the understanding of biblical prophecy and its fulfilment—not as the ultimate source of information on the economy, Y2K or related matters. If expert advice is needed, the services of a professional should be sought.

The publisher and author specifically disclaim any liability that is incurred from the use or application of the contents of this book.

TO
THE FAMILY
God has given
to my wife, Joyce,
and me

Brenda
Brent
Bonnie
Brad
Bryan
as well as to each member of their families.

Because of you, God has also given me
much love, joy, happiness, fun and many opportunities
to grow—through the difficulties
and disciplines that come
with the heavy, but welcome,
responsibilities of a family.

Contents

Author's Note

As is the case with any book which examines current events, *The Economy to Come* is out-of-date as soon as it is published.

This is particularly true of a volume that focuses on the economy, especially at a time when, as we go to press, the world economic scene is extremely volatile.

How can a prophecy author stay abreast of our rapidly changing world in terms of his books?

Well, apart from regular updates (which are only a partial solution), it is virtually impossible to be up-to-the-minute.

The proper approach, and the one which I have sought to follow since the first editions of both of my books on prophecy—*Apocalypse Next* in 1980 and *The Economy to Come* in 1983, which have gone into ten and four printings respectively—is to focus on the major biblical prophetic signs of end-time events. Obviously these have not changed since the first editions, for the Scriptures are forever settled.

Indications in current affairs of prophetic fulfillment do occur, increasingly so in my view. For this reason there have been periodic updates. These have *not* been revisions—the basics have not changed—but are simply attempts to compare what is currently happening in our world with what the Bible has predicted.

The best advice I can give any reader who wishes to be current in terms of prophetic fulfillment is this: Settle on what you are convinced, from Scripture, are the major indicators of prophesied end-time events. Then, be alert to events in our world which have a bearing on those indicators. Areas to particularly watch include:

- the nation of Israel
- the Islamic nations around her
- Russia
- movement toward a one-world government
- the church and the economy—coupled with increased invasion of privacy
- events related to the "birth pang" signs Jesus predicted

May you be blessed as you read these pages.

Sincere Thanks

- to the scores of people in many parts of the continent and abroad, especially to Danny Spivak, who have graciously shared with me much valuable material—newspaper articles, magazines, books, information;

- to Peter Lalonde, editor of *The Omega-Letter*, for permission to quote extensively from several issues;

- to Marilynne Foster, my skillful editor, whose expertise made this a better book;

- to Judy Harris whose skill at the computer keyboard was immeasurably helpful in producing this book in a timely fashion;

- to Dr. Gordon Cathey, esteemed pastor and counselor, for his careful assessment of the text;

- to a top-level government economist, who took the time to critique this manuscript and to affirm its essence;

and finally, to my friend K. Neill Foster whose encouragement and pressure continue to provide incentive and motivation to put my thoughts on paper.

Everything we know has an end, as well as a beginning. That the world, as we know it, should end is not at all improbable.

— K. Neill Foster

The Climax of Earth's Ages Is upon Us!

A nd the global economy plays a major role in that climax.
It's been predicted in sacred writings. An examination of
them forms a major thrust of this volume.

But first, a disclaimer. I am *not* an economist nor a financial
advisor. If you are looking for advice on investments, this
isn't the book for you.

However, if you want to explore what the Scriptures say
about the climactic events of planet earth in the light of economic realities and other factors, then read on.

Before we plunge into a look at how economics play a major role in prophetic fulfillment, let's take time for a brief
overview.

The End of the World!

People have been predicting it for centuries. As far back as
A.D. 156, in fact. The year A.D. 1000 was widely feared as a
global Doomsday. Again in A.D. 1260 a tremendous stir took
place in Europe as apocalyptic predictions became rife.

In the 1500s, Nostradamus, one of the best-known seers of
the past, made a number of amazing predictions in 1,050
verses, mostly quatrains. He has currently become a some-

what controversial figure, with literally hundreds of books being written about him and his prophecies in the past decade. A recent translation of his forecasts became a best-seller and the major topic of discussion in France—primarily because it was believed he had predicted the rise to power of socialism in that country as well as the assassination attempt on the Pope. Under Hitler's reign in Germany, Nostradamus' writings were banned because of his predictions (fulfilled for a time) of a divided Germany. These, and other apparently accurate prophecies, have caused multitudes to ask questions about the future and to examine what this sixteenth-century physician and astrologer has said.

I am not endorsing or affirming the prophecies of Nostradamus. His intriguing predictions and the incredible interest which they have aroused, especially in Europe, are cited merely as an illustration of the fact that such views are widely held and seriously considered.

Nostradamus is said to have predicted a climax to earth's affairs before the year 2000 according to *TIME* magazine.[1]

Fontbrune's *Nostradamus—Historian and Prophet* has the seer predicting a great war (World War III) after an earlier major conflict. *La Fin du Monde (The End of the World)*, a book published in France, details the results obtained by running the predictions of Nostradamus through a computer programmed to take into account the positions of the planets. Exact dates and locations for the coming disasters are said to result. The author, Maurice Chatelain, claims this reveals that the immediate future is full of wars, anti-Christs and natural disasters, though he says the 1999 date set by many Nostradamus buffs for the end of the world is wrong, predicting instead the year 3797.

Current Doomsday Predictions

Widespread terror concerning "Doomsday," as the media dubbed it on March 10, 1982, was reported around the world.

The fear arose as the result of predictions (later withdrawn) by a couple of scientists in their book, *The Jupiter Effect*. The book forecasts that the alignment of nine solar-system planets on our side of the sun would trigger earthquakes, violent weather and massive upheavals upon earth.

Of course, religious groups have regularly predicted the Apocalypse, setting it variously for 1844, 1914, 1915, 1975. Preachers through the years have frequently made similar prophecies the topic of hair-raising sermons.

Some years ago several obscure sects gained national publicity by setting specific dates for the return of Christ and the onset of the related awesome judgments predicted in Scripture.

More recently, widely publicized predictions have circulated. Over 3 million copies of the book *88 Reasons Why Christ Will Return in '88* were sold. (Understandably, the sequel, *89 Reasons . . .* , by the same author, did not sell so well.) A Korean group ran large ads in major newspapers around the world setting a date in the fall of 1993. A prominent U.S. Bible teacher, the owner of a chain of Christian radio stations, declared the fall of 1994 to be the time.

Unfortunately for the credibility of these self-styled prophets, all of their deadlines have come and gone and, quite obviously, Christ has not returned nor has the Apocalypse or Doomsday burst upon earth. Some of these groups, like the Jehovah's Witnesses, have attempted to save face by re-interpreting the coming of Christ to be an invisible advent or some other special arrival—a most unsatisfactory explanation.

So, when yet another voice is raised to suggest that the return of Christ and the attendant events that precede His final rule on earth really do appear to be near at hand, it's not unusual for people to respond with a skeptical, "We've heard all that before!"

Fair enough.

And very understandable.

But, in spite of the numerous false prophets with their widely publicized but inaccurate dating, the fact remains: The Bible does clearly predict that Jesus Christ will return to earth.

The Word of God (which lays claim to divine inspiration that can be abundantly verified) makes it clear that a brief but violent climax to earth's affairs *is* coming.

A Prophetic Overview

In a nutshell, the sequence of events is this. Believers in Christ all over the world will mysteriously disappear in the Rapture, sometimes called the "snatching away of the church." This will usher in a seven-year period Bible scholars call the Great Tribulation, with the final three-and-one-half years being the most awesome span in all of earth's history.

Not all students of biblical prophecy will agree with the position held by this author, since there are three major views concerning the end-time sequence of events:

1. One view holds that the return of Jesus Christ to earth will not occur until after a prophesied period of 1,000 years of peace called the Millennium.

2. Another view says that there will be no Millennium.

3. The third view is that the return of Christ precedes and precipitates the Millennium. This school of thought holds that the Rapture and the Tribulation both precede the Millennium, with the Rapture occurring at one of three times:

   (a) *before* the Tribulation (pre-Tribulation view),

   (b) *during* the Tribulation (mid-Tribulation view),

   (c) *after* the Tribulation (post-Tribulation view).

The author takes the pre-Millennium, pre-Tribulation position.

However, it should be noted that, regardless of the view held on the exact chronology of end-time events, all students of prophecy agree that an enormous catastrophic climax to human history is foretold. A bona fide "climax of the ages" is unquestionably to be found in mankind's prophetic writings!

A global dictator will arise. Famine, war, pestilence, earthquake activity and mind-boggling judgments (described in the Book of the Apocalypse—Revelation, last book of the Bible) will come upon earth. It will literally reel under the impact of these events.

The climactic battle of Armageddon, in which all nations of the world will participate, will be the final occurrence in this period. It will be precipitated by the revelation of Christ from heaven and the defeat of the forces of evil. Christ will then consign Satan to the abyss and establish His 1,000-year reign on earth—a reign with ideal conditions almost beyond human imagination.

What's the Evidence?

Now, what are the evidences for believing that this climax of the ages, which we'll describe in more detail later, is near? Can we be reasonable, intelligent individuals and still believe that it could happen soon? Or is all of this merely the wild-eyed ranting of deluded prophets whose fallacies have become clearly evident in numerous prophetic bloopers and blunders?

These are valid questions.

People do wonder: The world ponders the potential of a global economic collapse; concern mounts over the threat of a meltdown of human society resulting from the Y2K problem; a renewed fear of a nuclear arms race resurfaces; wars trouble our planet; the Middle East tinderbox creates widespread tension; and the fear of massive international nuclear terrorism grows.

Unfortunately, the concerns that fuel such questioning and uncertainty appear to be well-founded.

Outlook: Uncertain

Though the world went through a brief period of euphoria and optimism in the early 1990s after the collapse of the Soviet Union and the end of the Cold War, the reprieve was short lived.

In spite of the fact that, as then U.S. President George Bush announced, mankind was said to be building a "New World order of peace and prosperity," the harsh realities have been quite different.

Saddam Hussein's 1992 Gulf War, the aftermath of which is dragging on into the end of the decade, was a wake-up call to indicate that not much had changed in terms of global peace and brotherhood. The conflict in Bosnia (where World War II started), the ethnic cleansing massacres in several African nations, the internal violence in many countries and the specter of international terrorism—all are painful reminders that our world has not found its desired peace and security.

Consequently, many of the Cold-War-era fears have resurfaced. People recall predictions like that of China's Deng Xiaoping who said, "World War III is beyond man's capacity to avoid." Or articles such as Jonathan Schnell's *The New Yorker* piece: "The machinery of destruction is in place, poised on a hair trigger, waiting for the button to be pushed by some misguided or deranged human, or for some faulty computer chip to send out the instructions to fire." Such a suggestion takes on an added dimension of terror when it is recalled that *The New York Times* detailed thirty-two nuclear accidents involving weapons, admitted by the Pentagon, over a thirty-year period, any one of which "could have been the trigger to a chain reaction which would have turned the world into a massive nuclear crematorium."[2]

But Don't Despair

All of this could be more than a bit depressing. However,

The Economy to Come is a book of hope. In fact, if this volume were a highway, the appropriate sign would be: *There's Hope Ahead!*

Hang in there!

Notes

1 *TIME*, September 7, 1981, p. 23.
2 *The New York Times*, May 26, 1981, p. A1.

PART ONE

The Climax of the Ages

Economic Signs

"... the worst envisioned would be a global monetary collapse, triggered by energy shortages, and characterized by uncontrolled Weimar-style inflation that wipes out paper assets, beggars the middle class, and impoverishes everyone but the speculators."

— Canadian Business Magazine

> *"History is replete with examples of regulation and inflation leading to the worst type of political, social, moral, economic and military debacles. . . ."*
> —Douglas Casey in *Crisis Investing*

CHAPTER 1

A Basketful of Money for a Purseful of Groceries

It was August 14, 1923. Maria's birthday.

The worry lines etched themselves deeply into the face of the pretty German housewife . . . far too youthful at twenty-eight to be carrying in her features the evidence of such great anxiety.

After their meager breakfast, Maria had kissed her husband Hans good-bye, handing him an even more meager lunch as he set out for his day's work at the rail yards.

Alone now, she reflected on how unbelievably things had changed in the past year. There would be no birthday gift for her this year, not even something like the simple token of love Hans had managed last August.

Maria was frightened. What was happening to Germany? When was it all going to stop? Since the war had ended, the price of everything was increasing so fast it made her head swim. She just couldn't comprehend what was going on.

Wages Paid on the Hour

Yesterday Hans had told her that the workers at the rail yard had won the right to be paid on an hourly basis simply because the value of the currency was falling so rapidly that waiting even to the end of the day meant they were losing their purchasing power.

Now she would have to come to the rail yard fence each morning and afternoon. Hans would rush over and give her the salary, and she would go immediately to the shops and stand in line to purchase what food she could. Otherwise inflation would bite so deeply even in the course of an afternoon that they wouldn't be able to buy the bare necessities of life.

Maria let her mind run along the thought of birthdays. She reflected ruefully on how different it had been when Hans had his twenty-eighth birthday just last January. And the birthday before that in January of 1922.

Back then, only twenty months ago, she had been concerned about the cost of the eggs she bought to make Hans' birthday cake. In early 1922, an egg which had sold for a quarter of a mark at the end of the war in 1918 was selling for about 50 marks.

But now, only a year and a half later, eggs cost over 5,000 marks each! And everything else had gone up comparatively in price!

Maria fought the rising sense of panic which threatened to engulf her. Even the fact that Hans was now making nearly 15 million marks a week didn't help. The value of their money was dropping so fast that they just couldn't cope. She had to literally take a basketful of money just to get a few groceries!

What could they do? Nobody seemed to have an answer.

Suddenly Maria's self-control crumbled. She put her head down on the table and let loose a flood of despairing tears . . . a bitter birthday gift to herself.[1]

4

The kind of despair Maria experienced was common in the Germany of 1923, and many people tragically concluded that suicide was the only way out.

Little wonder.

The nation was in the grip of the most extreme case of inflation in history.

After World War I, the victorious Allies, particularly the French, demanded exorbitant redress from a German economy already shaken by the costly and unsuccessful war. Limits were set by the Allies on German industry in 1919, a reparations bill for 132 billion gold marks was submitted in 1921, and half of the Upper Silesian industrial area was given to Poland.

When the inexperienced left-wing German government was unable and unwilling to balance its budget, and the French army moved into the Ruhr in January of 1923 on a "mission of control" designed to squeeze the reparations out of German industry, the seeds of collapse were sown.

Passive resistance to the French and the closure of the factories were supported by the government through the printing of billions of new marks. The German unit of currency was well on its way to destruction.

The mark, which had traded at nine for one U.S. dollar in January 1919 had already declined steadily up to that time. It was sixty-five to one in January 1920 and 190 to one by January 1922. In July of 1922, it was 495 to one. At the time of the French squeeze in January 1923, it seemed to have hit the bottom at an astonishing exchange rate of 18,000 marks to one American dollar.

But, with added pressures and the government currency printing program, the slide became an almost vertical plunge. Stupendous denominations of currency were commonplace in Germany in 1923. Even though the presses were running around the clock, the bills were printed on one side only because there wasn't time to let the ink dry. As hyperinflation accelerated, billion- and trillion-mark notes became so common and so worthless that it was cheaper to paper a room with them than to use them to buy wallpaper.[2]

By July 1923, a single U.S. dollar was valued at 350,000 marks. In August it skyrocketed to 4,620,000. September saw an exchange rate of 100 million to one, and in October the rate was an incredible 25 billion marks to the dollar.[3]

In November 1923, before the nightmare came to an end, the exchange rate reached a number which only a mathematician could even contemplate: 4,200,000,000,000 (4.2 trillion) marks to a single dollar!

At that point, new "retenmarks" were issued—one for each inflated trillion-mark note. The middle class—those living on fixed incomes from salaries, pensions or investments—was wiped out. Many who had lived comfortably on investment income were literally paid off in full for the cost of a cup of coffee. They had to struggle desperately to stay alive, and some chose rather to end it all.

"Those who survived," says Jerome Smith in *The Coming Currency Collapse*, "were glad to listen to the promises of the National Socialists who were busy in Berlin as early as 1919. And thus the inflation from one war created the conditions which helped to bring about the next."[4]

This tendency of inflation and economic collapse to create conditions ripe for tyranny will, I believe, be multiplied a thousandfold in the climax of earth's ages toward which we are moving.

More Lessons from History

Though it is undoubtedly the most dramatic, the tragic German experience is not the only lesson from history concerning the effects of unchecked inflation.

The sad experience of an entire people during a series of paper money inflationary periods in medieval China from the ninth to the seventeenth centuries is traced in the *Swiss Economic Viewpoint*, October 1, 1976.[5]

In France also, from 1790 to 1796, the national currency, the *assignat*, hyperinflated to destruction. The guillotining of the royal family, anarchy and the rebellion of 1795, followed by Napoleon's seizure of power, were bitter fruits of that national financial experiment.[6]

Post-World War Italy, Poland and France are also sorry examples of massive inflation. Others include Brazil, Mexico and Argentina which demonstrate the enormously disruptive and long-lasting effects of inflationary policies in government.[7] The "Asian flu"—the late 1990's economic crisis in Japan and other Asian nations—is the most recent example.

Economic Blunders Continue

It is the opinion of numerous economists today that these historic inflationary disasters, as well as our current worldwide inflation, are the results of fundamental errors in government fiscal policy.

Most feel that these basic blunders continue to be perpetuated almost universally today.

Douglas Casey, in *Crisis Investing*, says:

> . . . a study of history can result in pessimism and cynicism when one realizes that government never, ever learns from history; it seems that the only thing we learn from history is the fact that we learn nothing from history.
>
> History is replete with examples of regulation and inflation leading to the worst type of political, social, moral, economic, psychological and military debacles; yet governments continue inflating, regulating and taxing.
>
> History may be viewed as a record of governments' various depredations upon their subjects.[8]

Casey's pessimistic conclusion, unfortunately, appears to be justified as we look around us today.

Such disastrous global economic mismanagement is unquestionably a major factor in creating the climate for the events we've been calling "the climax of earth's ages." But before we examine these, let's consider the current world economic outlook in more detail in Chapter 2.

Notes

1   Factual material for scenario excerpted from *The Coming Currency Collapse, Crisis Investing, After the Crash* and *The Eco-Spasm Report*.
2   Jerome Smith, *The Coming Currency Collapse* (Toronto: Bantam Books, 1981), p. 125.
3   Ibid., p. 126.
4   Ibid., p. 178.
5   Ibid., pp. 173-175.
6   Ibid., p. 179.
7   Ibid., pp. 185-187.
8   Douglas Casey, *Crisis Investing* (New York: Pocket Books, 1981), pp. 235-236.

*Could the sort of inflationary economic chaos that erupted
in Germany and other nations in the past ever occur again?
Is such an eventuality inconceivable—or could
it happen once more, this time on a global scale?*

CHAPTER 2

The Impending Global Economic Crunch

An amazingly high percentage of the best-sellers throughout North America in the past twenty years have been
pessimistic.

They are also books on the economy.

The overlap is not coincidental.

Glance at some of the titles: *Crisis Investing— Opportunities
and Profits in the Coming Great Depression; The Coming Currency
Collapse; Bankrupt; The Death of Economics; New Profits from the
Monetary Crisis* and *How to Prosper During the Coming Bad
Years.* There are many others of a similar nature, like *The
Coming Economic Earthquake, The Day the Dollar Dies* and *The
Cashless Society—World without Money.*

Most of these widely read books, as well as the numerous radio or television financial shows and economic newsletters, are
written or produced by bona fide economists or analysts—people like Jerome Smith, Harry Browne, Dr. Geoffrey Abert,
Howard Ruff, Larry Burkett, Alvin Toffler and others.

And, as we have indicated, all of them present a very gloomy economic outlook— on a global scale. Even those books whose forewords contain the disclaimer, "This is not a doomsday (or pessimistic) book," do so only on the basis that the authors believe that they can offer a way for their readers to prepare for and survive the coming bad times. None of the above-mentioned authors disagrees with the prediction that chaotic economic times are ahead.

Abert asks at the outset of his book:

What will you do when

- money is barely worth the paper it is printed on?

- transportation slows to a virtual halt?

- government services break down?

- cities default?

- banks close their doors?

- crime rises astronomically?

- the social fabric is ripped to shreds?

- and panic is everywhere?

This is not a science fiction nightmare. It is a sober scientific forecast based on unassailable facts. It is what you have to be prepared for.[1]

A number of these books have been around for a while. Some have been the object of ridicule, being scornfully dismissed as the work of "doomsday paranoics." But the potential for the fulfillment of much to be found in these writings seems greater than ever as the century draws to a close.

Fearful Forecast

The stark black and white cover on the October 12, 1998 issue of *Newsweek* was arresting.

But not just because of the bold graphics.

The title of the cover feature was the shocker: "Economy at Risk—The Crash of '99?" The subhead added, "It doesn't have to happen—but here's why it might."

The special report, produced by Robert J. Samuelson, was full of gloomy analysis of the global economic scene. Superimposed on a gripping graphic of a lineup of dominos (some of which are beginning to fall) was the record of a few of the events that lead to the situation in which a worldwide financial crisis is considered a distinct possibility. Those events include:

- The devaluation of the Thai currency in July 1997.

- The spread (in late 1997 and throughout 1998) of currency devaluations throughout all of Asia—including South Korea and Japan, the world's second largest economy. Latin America was affected as well.

- The subsequent tanking of world markets led to the Dow's largest one-day drop ever on October 27, 1997, after which it resumed its climb.

- In late spring of 1998 the Indonesian financial crisis precipitated massive widespread civil unrest, rioting and looting. The government was brought down by the crisis.

- The financial contagion spread to Russia and in the fall of 1998 the ruble plummeted. Moscow restructured (read "defaulted on") its debt.

- A giant U.S. hedge fund, the Long Term Capital Management L.P., was pushed to the brink of failure by the Russian crisis. It was saved only by a controversial Fed-led rescue which some analysts believe was the only thing that prevented a global economic meltdown.

- The U.S. economy, feeling the effects of the global woes, began to show signs of a slowdown.[2]

Samuelson wrote that what is occurring is a formula for depression. The pieces of the economy—consumption, exports/business investment, home building and government spending—do not appear to be capable of maintaining growth or preventing serious trouble.

In late 1998 the International Monetary Fund (which itself was in difficulty and needed U.S.-funded infusions of money) was announcing sharply reduced projections of world economic growth. Even those reduced projections were predicated upon healthy U.S. and European economies. The IMF forecast, with its qualifiers, plainly means, said Samuelson, "We don't know what will happen—and we're scared."

With the United States as "the last great domino propping up the world economy" the tremors are unnerving. Because, as the *Newsweek* article concluded, "If the U.S. falls, woe to us all."[3]

A Healthy U.S. Economy?

Can the "last great domino" hold steady?

Many financial analysts think so.

And yet, in spite of seven years of steady expansion (as this is written), the United States appears to be heading into unsettled and choppy economic waters.

Writing under the title "An Unfathomable Economy" in *U.S. News & World Report*, August 3, 1998, analyst James K. Glassman asked,

> So, which is it? (1) an economic slowdown that will lead to the first recession in seven years, (2) an acceleration of inflation, with the Federal Reserve slamming on the brakes and sending the stock market into the trash bin, (3) a continuation of the delightful "Goldilocks economy"—not too hot, not too cold, just right, or (4) something utterly unexpected?
>
> Correct answer: No one knows.[4]

Glassman indicated that the predictions in a survey of

economists were "all over the lot!" The chairman of the Federal Reserve Board, Alan Greenspan, was quoted as saying to the House Banking Committee: "I have been in the forecasting business for 50 years . . . and I know when I can forecast something reasonably well and not. This is a tough one."[5] And Glassman's article appeared before the crisis had deepened in Russia!

Larry Burkett, founder and president of Christian Financial Concepts, has authored a number of books on economic principles and personal finances. His 1991 best-seller, *The Coming Economic Earthquake*, predicted that fiscal calamity was on the horizon unless dramatic action was taken to restore financial sanity in government and commerce.

In a 1995 issue of his monthly newsletter *Money Matters*, Burkett quoted the then House Speaker Newt Gingrich as warning that the U.S. was headed for "fiscal crisis that will reach Mexican proportions [a speech at the time of the major Mexican economic crisis and bailout] by the year 2012."[6]

Unfortunately, little has been done since Gingrich's appeal. In spite of a "balanced budget" (more on this in the next chapter), the situation in the U.S., the "strongest, best performing economy in the world," presents a mixed bag.

Putting a Good Spin on It

As a background to an examination of the economy, it is important to consider the disturbing, but nonetheless real tendency of government to put the best possible political spin on financial and related matters. As an example of this, reflect on the following: One of the bright spots on the U.S. economic scene has been the reported labor and income statistics showing unemployment down and personal income up.

How reliable are these figures?

Unfortunately statistics provided by government are often suspect. For example, in a recent year the White House announced the creation of 760,000 jobs within the previous twelve-month period, with another 194,000 being created in a single month shortly thereafter, according to the U.S. Labor Department.

But when these claims were closely questioned by *Business Week* magazine, the Labor Department admitted that an astonishing 85 percent of those 194,000 jobs were created out of thin air without a shred of documentation. They further admitted that their normal monthly surveys of American companies detected only 29,000 new jobs. The 760,000 figure was obtained as the Clinton Administration "fudged" their figures by adding hundreds of thousands of imaginary jobs on the assumption that they may have missed some newly created positions in their surveys.[7]

Examples such as these give credence to the adage that there are two kinds of untruths: lies and government statistics. The downside is that confidence based on inaccurate figures can booby-trap an economy. Now, let's look at some specific disturbing indicators in the U.S. economy.

Notes

1   G. Abert, *After the Crash* (Scarborough: New American Library, 1979), inside front cover.
2   *Newsweek*, October 12, 1998, pp. 32-37.
3   Ibid., p. 37.
4   *U.S. News & World Report*, August 3, 1998, p. 48.
5   Ibid.
6   *Money Matters*, May 1995, p. 1.
7   As quoted in Grant Jeffrey, *Final Warning* (Eugene, OR: Harvest House Publishers), 1996, p. 347.

"Isn't it time we have an open dialogue about where we're going?"
—Former House Speaker Gingrich
during a 1998 budget debate

CHAPTER 3

The Warning Flags Are Flying

The ostrich, native bird of Australia, is famous for putting its head into the sand at the approach of danger. In this unsubstantiated belief, the bird is supposed to reason that if it can't see the danger, the danger will disappear!

Though ostriches don't actually do this, many people do engage in this kind of foolish, dangerous activity.

Some analysts suggest that this is what our culture is doing in regard to their personal as well as the national and international economy.

While it may seem more comfortable to ignore danger, a better course of action is to face it and take whatever action is possible or necessary.

In responding to the question posed in Chapter 2 as to whether the U.S. economy, which is "propping up the rest of the world," is up to such a task, it is important to realistically look at some of the danger signals.

1. *Monetized Debt.* Have you ever wondered how a govern-

ment, year after year after year, can spend more money than it takes in?

The answer is in the dangerously inflationary procedure of "monetizing the debt." Grant Jeffrey, in *Final Warning*, explains the process.

> Every year the U.S. federal government spends hundreds of billions more than it raises in taxes. [This statement was factual prior to the recent and rare budget surplus, which some believe was created in accounting and is actually a $28-billion deficit. "The No-Count Surplus," *Newsweek*, November 2, 1998, p. 45.] They make up the difference (the deficit) by borrowing money from the private sector, selling interest-bearing notes called treasury bills (T-bills) and bonds to investors.
>
> The banks buy these treasury bills from the U.S. Treasury to generate safe interest income. The U.S. Federal Reserve system will then buy back some of these bonds from the local banks.
>
> But where does the Federal Reserve find the money to do that? Believe it or not, they actually produce these dollars "out of thin air" in the Federal Reserve system computers.
>
> The Federal Reserve publishes its figures every Thursday, including a list of "U.S. Government securities bought outright." *The Wall Street Journal* reports that the Federal Reserve system buys between $1 and $2 billion worth of government debt every week. [Thus in a recent eighteen-month period] the Federal Reserve monetized government debt by purchasing over $90 billion of T-bills from the government.
>
> The Federal Reserve then allows the banks to use this money as new reserves. Using the three-to-one leverage provided by the fractional banking reserve system, the banks can use these new reserves as a basis to lend their customers huge new loans multiplied many times over

the amount of the actual reserves. When these loans are made to customers, the official bank assets increase thereby, and the money supply is also increased by this amount. Such financial "sleight-of-hand" transforms government debt into an increase in monetary supply. This "monetization" of government debt is the root cause of inflation—not the rise of wages and retail prices that inevitably follow such inflationary actions by the federal government.

Inflation robs us of our savings and makes economic planning and calculations almost impossible. Inflation punishes savers, such as long-term bond holders, and favors those who borrow money because they will ultimately repay their loans with inflated, cheaper dollars. Obviously, the greatest benefit is felt by the biggest debtor of all, the government. History reveals that inflation is government's favorite method of repudiating its debts.[1]

2. *Actual Inflation.* The official word is that inflation in the past decade in North America has been held to low single-digit figures.

A former Canadian Prime Minister claimed to have "wrestled inflation to the ground" during his term in office. Alan Greenspan, chairman of the Federal Reserve, has frequently adjusted interest rates in an effort to "maintain a low inflation rate."

Most people, if asked, would agree. Inflation is currently quite low.

But because the United States and Canada have gone off the gold standard (backing paper money with gold reserves) and because of the monetization of government debt (as described above) the real story is actually quite different.

The true picture of what hidden inflation does may be seen in the following graph.[2]

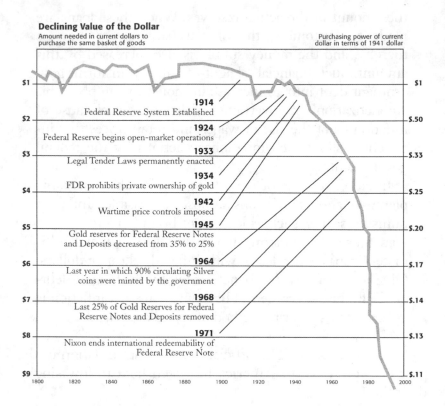

Declining Value of the Dollar

Amount needed in current dollars to purchase the same basket of goods

Purchasing power of current dollar in terms of 1941 dollar

1914
Federal Reserve System Established

1924
Federal Reserve begins open-market operations

1933
Legal Tender Laws permanently enacted

1934
FDR prohibits private ownership of gold

1942
Wartime price controls imposed

1945
Gold reserves for Federal Reserve Notes and Deposits decreased from 35% to 25%

1964
Last year in which 90% circulating Silver coins were minted by the government

1968
Last 25% of Gold Reserves for Federal Reserve Notes and Deposits removed

1971
Nixon ends international redeemability of Federal Reserve Note

And, ominously enough, a more direct form of inflation, such as occurred in Germany of the 1920s, has surfaced in Russia, when, along with its 1998 devaluation of the ruble, the government began the printing of an additional money supply.

In the U.S., the report that the Federal Reserve intends to increase the currency supply in 1999 as a safeguard against the millennium bug (Y2K) is disconcerting.[3] More on Y2K and its effect on the economy shortly.

3. *National Debt Crisis.* The official U.S. national debt, as of late 1998, stood at $5.5 trillion, growing at the rate of hundreds of billions a year. This total, however, does not include the more than one trillion dollars borrowed from the Social

Security trust fund or the unfunded government pension funds for civilian and military employees. If those amounts were included, the debt would be a staggering $8.8 trillion.

But even that isn't the full story.

Richard Lauren and Hank Brown, in an article entitled "The Best of Legislation, the Worst of Legislation," point out that the cost of the so-called "unfunded liabilities" for which the next generation will have to pay as the boomers age— military pensions, federal service pensions, increase in Social Security and Medicare—is staggering. They estimate that the cost of these benefits, along with the existing national debt, will total $17-19 trillion! They call this "the balanced budget lie" and claim that unless major action is taken quickly the result will be "national bankruptcy."[4]

The Canadian situation is little better, percentage-wise. Before recent major efforts to balance the budget, the national debt was over seventy-five percent of the Gross National Product.[5]

At some point, unless drastic action is taken, the governments of both the United States and Canada will hit the wall financially when the national debt and its compounding interest charges have risen to the point at which the total tax revenue will not be adequate to pay even the interest on the debt.

A nation cannot continue to borrow indefinitely. At some stage the only remaining options are economic collapse or hyperinflation which can only delay the ultimate. Governmental ability to print money, as Germany did in the 1920s and Russia has begun to do in 1998, creates a great temptation for politicians to start the printing presses in order to delay the inevitable collapse. It's a temptation as well because through hyperinflation a government can settle its national debt by "repaying" bondholders with inflated, devalued, basically worthless currency.

The warning flags are flying furiously throughout North America.

4. *Tax Burden.* Most North American citizens spend a major part of their year working for their governments. Tax freedom day—the day when the average citizen has earned enough to pay his annual taxes and can begin working for himself—is mid-May in the U.S. and early July in Canada where universal health-care adds a huge chunk to the tax load.

In one recent thirty-three-year period, according to the Frazer Institute in Canada, the tax burden of the average Canadian family rose by 1,200 percent. Income taxes and hidden taxes throughout North America are now the largest single family expenditure—more than housing, food and clothing expenditures combined.

Understandably taxation levels of this sort put tremendous pressure on any economy.

5. *Rising Rate of Bankruptcies.* Under the title "A Rising Tide of Bankruptcies Will Sink All Ships in the U.S. Economy," Lloyd Bentsen, former Secretary of the Treasury and Chairman of the Senate Finance Committee, issued a strong warning about the devastating effect the rapidly growing number of personal bankruptcies has on the economy. Citing statistics that indicated personal bankruptcies had more than doubled to a total of 1.2 million annually in the decade ending in 1996, Bentsen called for stronger legislation to prevent the "bankruptcy of convenience."[6]

Congress did attempt to act in late 1998 to make it more difficult to declare bankruptcy, particularly the kind in which people could repay a significant amount of the debt. But the legislation died.

So, the legacy of past years and the growing tendency to live beyond one's means and then leave creditors holding the bag through a declaration of bankruptcy is a tremendous drag on the economy. Personal and home equity debt, encouraged by easy credit, is at an all-time high in the U.S.[7]

The situation is almost the same in Canada. According to

Industry Canada, many households are just two paychecks away from bankruptcy.[8]

6. *Federal "Tinkering."* A cartoon in *The Washington Times* sums it up well. A nervous, perspiring car driver, labeled "Wall Street," is being directed by Alan Greenspan, his passenger: "Inflation ahead . . . deflation ahead . . . slow down . . . speed up!"

Greenspan, or whoever may be Chairman of the Federal Reserve Board, is indeed a powerful figure whose decisions are often called into question in terms of the good of the economy. Many observers feel that the degree of federal control is a dangerous thing.

In fact, the Federal Reserve system, which was established in 1914 by a group of the nation's leading bankers, has been called a "dishonest money system."

Steven Jacobson in "Money Control in America" writes:

> Use of the word "Federal" in the name "Federal Reserve" leads the public to believe that the Federal Reserve is a government institution. Contrary to this misleading use of language, the Fed (as it is commonly called) is a private corporation owned by domestic and foreign banks and operated for profit. The Fed controls the nation's money supply and interest rates and thereby manipulates the entire economy. This is actually in violation of Article 1, Section 8 of the United States Constitution which expressly charges Congress with "power to coin money and regulate the value thereof." Moreover, Article 1, Section 10 of the Constitution says: "No State shall make anything but gold and silver coin a tender in payment of debts."
>
> Gold and silver coins were taken out of circulation (in two stages ending in 1968), removed as backing for our currency and replaced with monetized debt—in other words, credit.
>
> . . . The definition of the word "dollar" has under-

21

gone a "newspeak" transformation to hide the fact that it is not money, but a unit of measurement for gold and silver coin. Title 12, United States Code, Section 152 states: "The terms 'lawful money' or 'lawful money of the United States' shall be construed to mean gold or silver coin of the United States." Title 31, United States Code, Section 371 says: "The money of account of the United States shall be expressed as dollars."

Unfortunately, contrary to the above, people have been led to believe that a dollar is both money and a measure of it. Perhaps a brief look at the history of money will help to clarify this.

Centuries ago, it became common practice for people to store their gold in the vault of the local goldsmith for a fee. The goldsmith would give the depositor a receipt for the amount of gold stored for safekeeping. The receipt was not money, but a money substitute. It also became common practice for people to exchange these "warehouse gold receipts" with one another for goods and services, as if they were money, since the receipts could be redeemed for the gold held in storage.

Let's assume that the hypothetical goldsmith soon discovered that only a small percentage of the gold stored in his vault was ever reclaimed at any given time. He began issuing receipts for more gold than he had, using some of them himself to buy things and loaning the rest at interest, while taking title to real property as collateral. In either case, there was no gold in the vault for these extra receipts. By increasing the quantity of the money substitute, the goldsmith stole from the holders of legitimate receipts, the value of which was reduced by the number of fraudulent receipts issued.

Paper currency, a money substitute, is honest only when the real money for which it is a substitute equals the number of receipts in circulation. Thus, by manipulating the number of receipts in circulation, the dishonest goldsmith quietly confiscated the wealth of the community without anyone being aware of what was happening. By reducing the number of receipts, he could make money scarce, causing a depression in which he could foreclose on property and increase his wealth. He could then stimulate economic activity and bring prosperity by increasing the number of receipts until the next cycle of plunder.

All of America's economic problems originate with the practice of issuing fraudulent receipts for gold that does not exist. This practice has become standard operating procedure for the banking establishment.

The modern day counterpart to the warehouse receipt for gold is the Federal Reserve Note. The word "Federal" implies Federal government, but the Federal Reserve is a privately owned corporation.[9]

The word "Reserve" implies that there is something to give the paper receipt value, but no gold or silver backs this paper. The word "Note" implies a contract, because a note by law must identify who is paying, what is being paid, to whom and when.

Between 1914 and 1963, Federal Reserve Notes never claimed to be money, nor did they claim to be dollars. A note for five dollars read: "The United States of America will pay to the bearer on demand five dollars." To the left of the President's picture and above the bank seal, it said: "This note is legal tender for all debts public and private, and is redeemable in lawful money at the United States Treasury or at any Federal Reserve Bank."

In 1963, soon after the assassination of President Kennedy, the Fed began to issue its first series of notes without the promise, while removing from circulation notes with the promise. To the left of the President's picture and above the bank seal, it now reads: "This note is legal tender for all debts public and private."

[On the new Treasury bills issued in 1998, even the word "Bank" has been removed. No longer does the seal state that the note is issued at some particular Federal Bank. The new note simply indicates it is issued by The Federal Reserve *System* (emphasis mine).]

By removing the promise to redeem the note in lawful money, the Federal Government, in cooperation with the Federal Reserve, eliminated the monetary system of the United States as established by the Constitution and replaced it with something totally different.

"Keeping Our Money Healthy," a publication of the Federal Reserve Bank of New York, states on page 12 that ". . . the Federal Reserve System works only with credit." Credit is not a tangible substance. The only thing that gives paper money value is the confidence people have in it. It is entirely psychological.

An honest money system uses wealth as a medium of exchange. Wealth is physical, not psychological. People produce wealth through their labor, transforming natural resources into usable products that have exchange value in the marketplace.

Centuries ago, when the goldsmith issued his first receipt for gold that did not exist, he created credit. He also created inflation, because credit and inflation are the same thing—receipts for wealth that does not exist.

It was Daniel Webster who said: "Of all the contrivances devised for cheating the laboring classes of mankind, none has been more effective than that which deludes him with paper money."[10]

Though few people realize it, the Federal Reserve System is the present-day counterpart of the goldsmith in the above illustration. It enables control of the economy by a small elite.

7. *The Coming Stock Market Crash.* "There's Reason for Worry on Wall Street." Thus nationally syndicated columnist and former presidential candidate Pat Buchanan headlined his May 4, 1998 column in *The Washington Times*. Pointing out that, at the time he wrote, the Dow had soared sixty-five percent in two years, with stocks selling at twenty-eight times their earning power, Buchanan noted that stocks were less an investment than an enormous gamble.

He quoted *The Economist's* call for higher interest rates: "In the late 1920's [just before the Great Depression], the Fed was also reluctant to raise interest rates in response to surging share prices leaving rampant bank lending to push prices higher still. When the Fed did belatedly act, the bubble burst with a vengeance."

Buchanan concluded with a dramatic warning:

Though these ominous warnings from such respected voices may not be well received in today's euphoria, they need to be taken seriously. For if they are right, America is headed for serious economic turbulence, and it is not far off.

To this writer, *The Financial Times* and *The Economist* are speaking painful but necessary truth.

The U.S. economy may be the strongest and freest on Earth, the marvel of mankind, but all these U.S. companies simply cannot be worth all that money. Like Wile E. Coyote of the "Roadrunner" cartoons, the Dow can defy the laws of gravity only so long.

Yet the optimism endures. *The Economist* quotes an editorial from *Forbes* magazine that eerily mirrors the hubris of the present: "For the last five years, we have been in a new industrial era in this country. We are making progress industrially and economically not even by leaps and bounds but on a perfectly heroic scale." So wrote Forbes in June, 1929, *four months before the crash* [emphasis mine].[11]

8. *Banking Crisis.* To understand the potential banking crisis in America it is essential to grasp the concept of fractional reserve banking.

A succinct explanation by Mike Phillips, posted during CompuServe's Year 2000 forum, gives the picture:

> . . . [T]here's really only one point you need to grasp to understand everything you need to know: the money's not there. The average person generally thinks that if he deposits $1,000 in his bank, the bank keeps it until he needs it. A more sophisticated person probably realizes that in order to pay interest, even on his checking account, they must lend it out to earn the interest. Having heard about reserve requirements and that they're about 20 percent, he assumes they keep $200 and lend out $800.
>
> Both are wrong. What the bank actually does is send the entire $1,000 to the Federal Reserve. Then, having reserves of $1,000, they proceed to make loans of $5,000, which are shown as a deposit in the borrower's checking account. Thus, the loan is both an asset and a liability to the bank and the books balance. This is the mechanism that the government, in conjunction with the banks, uses to create money. They don't run the printing presses anymore. The purpose of the Federal Reserve is to coordinate this process, making sure all banks create money, or inflate, at the same rate.
>
> If this is your first exposure to this subject, you probably think, This is crazy. How can this work? I don't just deposit money in my checking account to leave it there. What happens when I spend it? The key is that it works as long as the money never leaves the system. [Consider. A depositor withdraws money and spends it. The business where it was spent in turn deposits it in a bank.] The cash never really leaves the banking system, at least not permanently. The government prints just

énough paper money to support the demand for cash, and it is constantly recycled in and out of the banks. Over 90 percent of our fiat money [money not convertible into coin] is computer entries and because of the fractional reserve banking system, even that isn't there. It's been loaned out at the rate of five dollars for every dollar of deposits.

So, what would happen if lots of people decided to withdraw their money in cash and not spend it? That's when the system will collapse. First of all, there isn't that much paper money in existence, just enough to support the current demands. Before it could be given out, it would first have to be printed. But even that wouldn't solve the problem. The banks have allowed for the current small amount of currency usage, but the rest of the money is over at the Federal Reserve acting as deposit for the pyramid loan structure. In order to pay money to its depositors, it would first have to call in loans, five dollars for every dollar a depositor wanted. But, they really can't do this either. For the banks have committed the cardinal sin of banking— borrowing short and lending long. . . .

Proclaiming that a fiat money system will collapse does not really qualify as much of a prediction. . . . Every fiat money system in recorded history has collapsed. . . . Anyway, it's one thing to predict the collapse of a fiat money, fractional reserve banking system. "When" is something else. Our money system is like one of those cartoon characters that have run off a cliff and are still running in mid-air. Our fiat money is still convenient, consistent, easily divisible and most important, accepted. However, it is accepted out of habit, not because it has any inherent value. . . .

This acceptance is a state of mind and it can change in a heartbeat.

It did in the Great Depression of 1929-30. People went from drinking and dancing at the speakeasies to lining up at the doors of closed banks in a short period of time. The catalyst was the failure of a bank in Austria, of all places! They began calling in loans, other European banks followed and eventually they started calling in loans with American banks. Once an inverted pyramid begins to collapse, it takes on a life of its own. The problem is predicting the triggering event.

That's where Y2K comes in. [Some have thought that the Y2K event could be such a trigger.] It has the potential, in many ways, to put an exact time on what heretofore has been unpredictable. . . . [12]

Only time will tell whether Y2K, or some similar event, proves to be the catalyst that causes the failure of our money as we now know it. But as all past fiat systems have, it will fail at some point. It's interesting to note that Jesus used the phrase "*when* [your money] fails . . . ." Not *if*, but *when* (Luke 16:9, KJV).

We're Insured, Aren't We?

"But," someone protests. "What about the FDIC? It insures deposits, doesn't it?"

The Federal Deposit Insurance Corporation (FDIC) was created by Congress in 1933 and now does indeed insure bank deposits up to $100,000 per customer for member banks. It is, however, a voluntary system and over 500 U.S. banks are not members. More serious is the fact that, during the recent savings and loan crisis, the FDIC was overwhelmed with claims and had to be directly bailed out by the government at a cost to taxpayers of $700 billion.

In spite of that warning, the FDIC remains massively underfunded, with assets of approximately $1 billion to insure $4 trillion in over 14,000 bank and S&L accounts.

9. *Y2K Potential Problems.* As suggested in the previous section, the year 2000 could present, in the opinion of some, massive worldwide problems and serve as the trigger to cause the collapse of our fiat money system.

Writers C. Lawrence Meador and Leland G. Freeman suggest one of the reasons for such a view—the ripple effect:

> It's the first week of the year 2000, and you're heaving great sighs of relief. All of your systems are functioning properly. The big bucks you spent on analyzing, fixing, and replacing your million lines of code was money well spent.
>
> But what you don't realize is that one of your suppliers didn't fare so well, and just-in-time [JIT] shipments of parts that should have left that supplier's factory on Monday didn't. Tomorrow, three of your plants will shut down for want of that part. Your JIT shipments to your biggest customer won't happen, causing your customer to default on an important government contract.
>
> Excuse me, but the CEO wants to see you—now![13]

Michael Hyatt in *The Millennium Bug* quotes a warning issued by Leon Kappleman and Phil Scott in *ComLinks.Com* magazine:

> The world has become extremely dependent on computer technology. Many benefits have resulted, but this dependency is not without risks. . . . Computer failures have been responsible for seriously interfering with, and even stopping, the delivery of products and services in health care, banking, security exchanges, retail, manufacturing, telecommunication, air traffic control and electric utilities, to name but a few. What would happen if suddenly all of those computers began to malfunction? The global economy would come to a screeching halt.[14]

And of course there's always the possibility of Y2K-compliant systems being affected by those that are non-compliant, like a virus. The Gartner Group, one of the most highly respected and widely quoted Y2K research groups in the world, points out;

> A program can fail in one of two ways. The first is simply when a program stops working and the failure is recognized immediately. The second, more insidious, is for the program to continue to run, generating false information, thus spreading the equivalent of a "virus."[15]

To Sum It Up

These then, are some of the danger signs that cause concern over the state of the United States' economy and, coincidentally, the world's: inaccurate statistics, monetized debt, hidden inflation, burgeoning national debt, heavy taxation, Federal Reserve machinations, an overblown stock market, the potential banking crisis and Y2K.

This list does not exhaust the catalog of troubling factors confronting the U.S., "the last great domino propping up the world economy." Allen Sinai, chief economist at Primark Global Economies, hailing a surprise U.S. interest rate cut on October 16, 1998, reinforced the connection between the U.S. and world economies when he said, "If the United States goes, the world goes. If the United States stands, the world stands."[16]

The Danger Is Real

Obviously, to suggest that there is the very real danger of a global economic collapse is not at all in the realm of the ridiculous or the implausible.

Treasury Secretary Robert Rubin, in an interview with *USA Today*, October 16, 1998, was asked if he saw any progress in battling the global economic crisis. While he was cautiously optimistic, Rubin said ". . . the [global] problems developed over a long time, and it will take time to work them out. We need to be realistic about the great difficult challenges that lie ahead in terms of working out all of these problems."

Asked later if he was optimistic, he replied, "I'm neither optimistic nor pessimistic. I just think it's critical that [global rescue and reform efforts] happen."[17]

Indeed, the crisis of 1999 appears to be too massive for any one nation, even the ostensibly powerful U.S., to handle. The solution must come through international effort.

Is There a Conspiracy to Rule the World Financially?

Any reference to international financial organizations, agreements or units immediately raises, in the minds of many thoughtful people, at least two major questions.

First, is there (as has been so often suggested) a shadowy global conspiracy by the wealthy elite of earth to totally control the entire world through its economy? And second, if there is such a conspiracy, how does the present dismal economic picture fit into its plans? Have our current worldwide economic difficulties come about through the conspirators' design? Or has the present situation taken them by surprise and, as a result of their manipulation or ignorance or inability, is the world economy totally out of the control of anyone?

Let me answer these two vital questions directly and briefly in Chapter 4, then provide the documentation for my responses.

Notes
1 Grant Jeffrey, *Final Warning* (Eugene, OR: Harvest House Publishers, 1996), pp. 351-353.
2 "A Rare Opportunity Awaits You," *Swiss America Corporation*. Chart based on material prepared by George Edward Durell Foundation, pp. 10-11.
3 *USA Today*, August 20, 1998, p. B1.
4 R. Lauren and H. Brown, "The Best of Legislation, the Worst of Legislation," *Christian Century*, December 3, 1997, Vol. 114, No. 34, pp. 1122-1125.
5 *Macleans*, April 20, 1996, p. 20. The interest on such debt is stagger-

ing—hundreds of billions of dollars per year in the U.S. . . . nearly $2 billion per day.

   To get a handle on how much $1 billion is, consider this illustration, culled from an Ann Landers' column: A man gave his wife $1 million. He told her to go out and spend $1,000 a day. She did. Three years later, she returned to ask for more money because the million was spent. He then gave her $1 billion and told her to spend $1,000 a day. She didn't come back for 3,000 years. But remember that we're talking trillions—not billions. We're talking about multiplying things indicated in the illustration by 1,000!

6 *The Patriot News*, Harrisburg, PA, December 12, 1997, p. A19.

7 *The Washington Times National Weekly Edition*, May 4-10, 1998, p. 39.

8 *Macleans*, May 15, 1996, p. 41.

9 Actually, the Fed is a quasi-government institution by design. The chairman is appointed by the President and Board members elected by the regional Reserves. At its establishment by Congress in 1914, it was made independent of government to serve as a firewall between the political world that wants "easy" money and the financial sector.

10 Steven Jacobson, "Money Control in America," *Real Money Perspectives*, Vol. VIII, Issue IV, 1995, pp. 1-10.

11 Patrick Buchanan, "There's a Reason for Worry on Wall Street," *The Washington Times National Weekly Edition*, May 4-10, 1998, p. 39.

12 Mike Phillips (75557.232@compuserve.com) "Y2K and Banks," CompuServe's Year 2000 Forum, 24 September 1997. Used by permission.

13 C. Lawrence Meador and Leland G. Freeman, "Year 2000: The Domino Effect," *Datamation*, January 1997, as quoted by Michael Hyatt in *The Millennium Bug*, p. 44.

14 Leon Kappelman and Phil Scott, "What Management Needs to Know About the Year 2000 Computer Date Problem," as quoted by Michael Hyatt in *The Millennium Bug*, p. 47.

15 The Gartner Group, "The Domino Effect of Hidden Year 2000 Problems," Research Notes, *Key Issue Analysis*, March 13, 1997.

16 *The Patriot News*, October 16, 1998, p. A1.

17 *USA Today*, October 16, 1998, p. B2.

> *"This myth [of a conspiracy to rule the world], like all fables, does in fact have a modicum of truth. There does exist, and has existed for a generation, an international Anglophile network. . . ."*
>
> —Professor Carroll Quigley in *Tragedy and Hope*

CHAPTER 4

Yes, Virginia, There Probably Is a Conspiracy

The questions posed at the end of Chapter 3—whether there is a conspiracy to rule the world financially and, if so, how the current economic morass fits in—are significant queries.

They deserve thoughtful answers.

First, I have come to believe as a result of my research that there is good evidence to support the view that a conspiracy to create a one-world financial state could indeed exist.

Though I will attempt to support and explain this conviction in a moment, I must say at the outset that I do not believe the motives of the alleged conspirators to be inherently and necessarily evil as some have charged.

Second, I frankly confess that I do not know whether the current and projected global economic disaster is engineered or by accident. In my judgment, a fairly good case can be made for either position, but, as we will explain later in this chapter, it really doesn't matter. In the final analysis, the effect is the same. And that effect, I am convinced, has been clearly foretold in the prophetic writings. More on that later.

Why Do I Believe There May Be a Conspiracy?

I must preface my response by saying that for years I tended to reject, almost out-of-hand, the material that kept coming across my desk about a mysterious global financial conspiracy. So much of it was extreme, poorly documented and, in some cases, badly written.

I agree with the opinion expressed by Ron Marr, editor of *The Christian Inquirer*, in this regard, when he wrote in *New World Order—Special Report*:

> Frankly, the inflammatory rhetoric of many writers claiming to know the secrets of worldwide conspiracy dating back to the Illuminati in 1776, to Machiavelli in the 1300s and to occult traditions in the early days of mankind tends to turn me off.
>
> So do the findings of those who lay all of our problems at the door of a communist conspiracy or a Zionist conspiracy or a Masonic conspiracy.[1]

However, as I have read and researched material like Marr's *New World Order*, Hal Lindsey's *Countdown to Armageddon*, *Mystery 666* by Don Stanton, *The Naked Capitalist* by Cleon Skousen, *Tragedy and Hope* by Carroll Quigley, and others, I have become convinced that there appears to be an international, non-governmental group of financiers, intellectuals, industrialists and politicians whose goal is the development of a one-world government, one-world bank and a one-world currency. This "conspiracy," according to Ron Marr, is not to be understood as being a single, unified plot:

> It appears much more likely that the dynamic direction which has so evidently emerged in this century is the result of many planners in pursuit of world domina-

tion from very different perspectives and purposes, each attempting to use the other—each in the hope that they will emerge as the ultimate controlling force.[2]

Though it is no doubt true, as Marr says, that there are many independent—even competing—elements at work in any quest for world domination, one particular agency is especially significant and is worthy of our special attention. That group is the Trilateral Commission.

The Trilateral Commission: How Does It Fit In?

Very few people are aware even of the existence, let alone the purposes, of the Trilateral Commission. Hal Lindsey, in *Countdown to Armageddon*, says that only one or two percent of his audiences in recent years have indicated to him even an awareness of the existence of the Commission.

Lindsey admits to being baffled by this in view of the fact that the Commission is an "international non-elected group of the western world's most powerful bankers, media leaders, scholars and government officials bent on radically changing the world." The changes which this group envisions, without obtaining permission to make such changes from any of earth's people through the ballot box, will, according to Lindsey, affect the individual and economic status of every person in the world.[3]

Let me attempt to document that last statement.

To Start at the Beginning

The obvious need for some kind of system to regulate international trade has always existed.

Prior to World War II, control of world trade was achieved primarily through the posting of tariffs by Britain, France, Holland, Portugal and the United States. These tariffs, under the imperial system, made it difficult for nations outside to trade with citizens inside. Thus, international control was maintained.

However, it became apparent during World War II that the system could not survive in the post-war era. Plans for a replacement system were developed in 1944 by John Maynard Keynes, an outstanding British economist, and Harry Dexter White, another brilliant economist from the United States.

These plans came to be known as the Bretton Woods system, a name taken from the small New Hampshire town in which they were developed.

The Bretton Woods agreement sought to solve two problems:

1. The manipulation of national currencies by their governments so as to protect their own currency and weaken those of other nations, resulting in worldwide financial instability.

2. The problem of protective tariffs, raised indiscriminately by nations or groups of nations, resulting in closed markets to the underdeveloped nations and the inhibiting of free international trade.

Fixing currency exchange rates was seen as the solution to the first problem. To achieve this required the establishment of two international institutions—the International Monetary Fund (IMF) and the World Bank. In addition to setting currency exchange rates, these two institutions were given, by agreement, authority to provide credit to the world's "have not" countries and to lend money to nations ravaged by war.

The establishment of the most-favored-nation system of trade was the proposed solution to the tariff problem. Under this scheme, underdeveloped nations which had difficulty competing for international trade were granted this status and were exempt from paying tariffs. Freedom from tariff payments meant that such nations could offer their goods more cheaply, and so international trade was stimulated.

The General Agreement on Tariffs and Trade (GATT) is the international pact which controlled this system.

But any system can be violated, and the success of the Bretton Woods plan depended upon some power capable of enforcing its provisions.

The Enforcer

The United States was the logical choice to provide that control. In 1944 the U.S. dollar was already the basic world currency: It was stable, backed both by the gold standard and a healthy economy.

In addition, the United States at that time consumed more than half of the world's total exported goods and thus was in a position to regulate GATT. As the greatest economic power in the world, the U.S. could also effectively deal with violators of the system, using tariff restrictions or credit control to punish infractions.

Bretton Woods greatly encouraged free trade. It did not tamper with the sovereignty of nations, working instead on the basis of a community of nations. Under it, the world witnessed the greatest growth in international trade in all human history—from virtually nothing at the end of the war, to over $400 billion by the early 1970s.

Oh! Oh!

But, beginning in the decade of the 1960s, the "enforcer"—the United States—began to stumble, and Bretton Woods started to fail. Here's how it happened.

An increasing deficit in the U.S. balance of payments and the removal of the gold standard robbed the American dollar of its stability and power.

Japan, resurgent after the war, and the increasingly powerful European Common Market became strong competitors to the U.S. in the international marketplace. The result was a weakened U.S. ability to deal with GATT violators.

Third World countries were increasingly forced to limit their trade because of their inability to pay. Many observers feel that it was this lack of Third World purchasing power that finally brought an end to Bretton Woods.

Writing in *The Christian Science Monitor*, economist Jeremiah Novak says that the demise of the Bretton Woods system "was [finally] precipitated by . . . [President] Nixon . . . in 1971, when the United States devalued the dollar and imposed a tariff surcharge on imports."[4]

Numerous unsuccessful attempts[5] by various groups to revamp the Bretton Woods system made it very clear that a new arrangement was necessary.

Such an arrangement was soon forthcoming.

In July, 1973, David Rockefeller recruited some 200 leading international bankers, businessmen, politicians and labor leaders to join him in research into the complex problems faced in international affairs.

Zbigniew Brzezinski (Special Presidential Advisor for National Security during the Carter administration), who was then Columbia University's specialist on international relations, was handpicked by Rockefeller to be the key intellectual in the formulation of the policies of this new system.

A Vision

What Rockefeller envisioned was the Trilateral Commission. *Newsweek* described the Commission's inception in these words: ". . . The Trilateral Commission, a brainchild of David Rockefeller, was transformed into reality by Zbigniew Brzezinski."[6]

He and Rockefeller attracted some of the top intellectuals of Japan, Europe and the United States to join in the task of reshaping world economics.

Senator Barry Goldwater wrote: ". . . Zbigniew Brzezinski and David Rockefeller screened and selected every individual who was invited to participate in shaping and administering the new world order."[7]

The name "trilateral" was adopted because the Rockefeller/

Brzezinski task force decided that the basis for a new world economic order would have to be the United States, the European Common Market and Japan acting in unison. Because these three entities together represented seventy percent of world trade, they therefore had, in the minds of the Commission, the "right and duty" to create a new system. More than this, they had the power (which the U.S. alone now lacked) to enforce any replacement for Bretton Woods.

Thus the three spheres of economic influence and power were to be combined into one force—the Trilateral Commission.

Jeremiah Novak said:

> The group believes that the policies of the trilateral world must be harmonized, as the U.S. alone can no longer take on responsibility for the international economic system. It also believes that if a new order is created, it must be based on a recognition that the U.S. is now only the first among equals in the industrial world. . . . As a result of this conclusion, U.S. foreign policy must undergo a transformation of gigantic proportion.[8]

It appears that the direction here indicated fits in with the "one-world" concept which certainly involves the continued lowering of the U.S. leadership profile in the world. Brzezinski himself wrote in the Council on Foreign Relations publication *Foreign Affairs:*

> ". . . the world is not likely to unite willingly behind a common ideology or a superpower. The only practical hope is that it will now respond to a common concern for its own survival . . . the active promotion of such trilateral cooperation *must now become the central priority of U.S. policy."* [emphasis mine][9]

Novak went on to show, in his *America* article, that the areas which the Trilateral Commission claims the right to regulate are far greater than those dealt with by Bretton Woods.

He wrote:

> The rules cover such areas as international monetary systems, international trade in raw materials and industrial goods [a new area not covered in Bretton Woods] and use of "commons," such as the oceans, space and the (north and south) poles. These rules are seen as universally applicable and subject to sanctions in the event they are violated.[10]

Just exactly how the Commission expected to enforce the international monetary rules is the subject of Chapter 5.

Notes

1 *The Christian Inquirer: A New World Order—Special Report*, June 1980, p. 2.
2 Ibid., p. 2.
3 Material drawn from H. Lindsey, *Countdown to Armageddon* (New York: Bantam Books, 1981); D. Stanton, *Mystery 666* (India: privately published, 1980) and various issues of *American Opinion*.
4 *The Christian Science Monitor*, February 7, 1977, p. 16.
5 One such step was the creation in March 1969 of a new medium exchange—Special Drawing Rights (SDR). Don E. Stanton, in *Mystery 666*, explains:

> The world was given a little insight into the future monetary system on March 31, 1969, when the IMF (International Monetary Fund) announced that the nations were ready to start business, using a new type of exchange which would eventually replace all other currencies and even gold. This new medium was referred to as "Paper Gold," but it is neither paper nor gold. It is a number/credit system of Special Drawing Rights (SDR).

> This was a big step forward, and on that same day, Pierre Schweitzer declared, "Gentlemen, we are right on schedule." In 1976 the IMF declared that gold would be re-

placed by SDR as the reserve of the Fund. Since then the Fund has been auctioning off its gold holdings.

SDR are simply numbers in the international "books" which represent the credit of the member nations. SDR are now being used for international trade. No currency is used, but the account of the nation is debited or credited for purchases or sales. SDR presents a unified unit for international trade. Existing currencies have a value in relationship to SDR—for instance, one SDR may be worth $1.20 on the IMF books.

Eventually, however, all currencies will become obsolete and canceled. SDR will then be the means for transactions for all individuals as well as nations. Naturally if the leading nations adopt the system (and they are doing that step by step) then all nations must follow. The only alternative would be complete isolation from world trade.

The changeover can be seen in many areas already. From 1977 on, airlines have been quoting passenger fares and cargo rates in SDR. The OPEC oil countries are considering an SDR pricing system.

The need is, however, not merely for a unified currency but for an instantaneous means of payment (other than handling over cash on the spot). SDR, of course, can't be "handed over," for they are numbers. They can only be debited or credited in the "books." And the "books" are not ordinary books, but computers.

SDR, though not the solution sought, are nevertheless an integral part of the "New Order."

D. Stanton, *Mystery 666* (India: privately published, 1980), p. 53.

6 *Newsweek*, June 16, 1975, p. 45.
7 As quoted by H. Lindsey in *Countdown to Armageddon*, p. 122.
8 Ibid.
9 *Foreign Affairs*, July 1975, p. 31.
10 As quoted by H. Lindsey, op. cit., p. 123.

*". . . [A]ny conclusion that there is no Conspiracy
out to rule the world is simply asinine."*
—Alan Stang in "Proofs of a Conspiracy"

CHAPTER 5

No Time for a Political Vacuum

Having determined the basis on which the international economic system ought to operate, the Trilateral Commission sought the ways and means to make it happen.

A Political Platform Needed

The Commission recognized that there had to be provisions made for relations with the communist (then in control of a large percentage of earth's peoples), Third World and OPEC nations in its bid to make the world economically interdependent. It is apparent they did not expect their system to exist in a political vacuum.

Indeed not.

They handpicked certain of their members to be groomed for the highest political offices in their respective home nations—especially the United States, which was and is still a major world leader in terms of power and influence.

An article in the *Atlantic Monthly* stated: "Although the Commission's primary concern is economic, the Trilateralists pinpointed a vital political objective: To gain control of the American presidency."[1]

An example of how this is believed to be played out is seen in the 1976 U.S. presidential election.

Georgia's first-term Democratic governor, Jimmy Carter, impressed Rockefeller by establishing a trade agreement with Japan for his state. Already contemplating a run for the presidency, Carter was very responsive to the Commission's interest. He later said "the Commission was a splendid learning opportunity."[2]

Carter's ambition matched the Commission's needs which were described thus in *U.S. News & World Report*: "The [Commission] founders, anxious to have a liberal Southerner in their ranks, invited Jimmy Carter, then the governor of Georgia, to join them."[3]

And so Carter, after becoming a charter member in 1973, received a thorough indoctrination in Trilateralist views from none other than Brzezinski himself.

The rest is history.

A virtual political unknown, Jimmy Carter came out of nowhere with the unquestioned backing of the enormously powerful Trilateralists in the news media to capture the White House.

He soon rewarded that support.

U.S. News & World Report made this comment shortly after Carter took office:

> The Trilateralists have taken charge of foreign policy-making in the Carter administration, and already the immense power they wield is sparking some controversy. Active or former members of the Trilateral Commission now head every key agency involved in mapping U.S. strategy for dealing with the rest of the world.
>
> Altogether, 16 high posts in the administration are held by men and women associated with the organization. Some see this concentration of power as a conspir-

acy at work.[4]

A similar situation exists elsewhere in Japan and Europe. Economist Novak says: "Its [the Commission's] membership roster reads like a Who's Who in business, labor and [Trilateral nation] government."[5]

Hal Lindsey, in *Countdown to Armageddon* writes:

> It's been interesting to me to watch various news media heavyweights rush to defend the Commission against charges that it has gained undue power in the world's governments.
>
> In general, they publish articles which minimize the Commission's influence, characterizing its members as a bunch of frustrated and powerless armchair idealists who wish they could institute some of their ideas in world affairs. . . . [They] call it simply a floating study group with no essential power, and they label the Commission's critics as isolationist conservatives or Marxist-leaning leftists.
>
> I wonder if the fact that so many news media executives are also Commission members has anything to do with these published defenses.
>
> For the media to say that the Trilateral Commission has no essential political power, however, is an insult to the intelligence of the American public. It also assumes that most Americans didn't read or don't remember the many articles which detailed the Commission's growing power and were published in those same newspapers and magazines in the 1977 era.[6]

Who Really Runs the World?

Not only is there evidence that the Trilateralists have successfully sought international power, but also that the Commission has a close tie with a political entity holding a similar view, one which focuses on U.S. foreign policy.

This group, known as the Council on Foreign Relations (CFR), is a private, non-elected group incorporated in 1921. Its present headquarters is the Harold Pratt House in New York City.

The extent of the CFR's influence and its relationship to the Trilateral Commission is highlighted by the words of CFR President Winston Lord: "The Trilateral Commission doesn't secretly run the world. The Council on Foreign Relations does that."[7]

In 1939, the CFR approached the U.S. State Department and offered its services in terms of advice and aid in international affairs. Their efforts were financed by the Rockefeller Foundation.

The late Senator Barry Goldwater revealed:

> From that day forward the Council on Foreign Relations has placed its members in policy-making positions with the federal government, not limited to the State Department.
>
> Since 1944 every American Secretary of State, with the exception of James F. Byrnes, has been a member of the CFR.
>
> I believe the CFR and its ancillary elitist groups are indifferent to communism. They have no ideological anchors. In their pursuit of a new world order they are prepared to deal without prejudice with a communist state, a socialist state, a democratic state, monarchy, oligarchy—it's all the same to them.
>
> Rear Admiral Chester Ward of the U.S. Navy (retired), who was a member of the CFR for 16 years, has written, "The most powerful cliques in these elitist groups have one objective in common—they want to bring about the surrender of the sovereignty and the national independence of the United States."[8]

Rear Admiral Ward quotes the president of Yale University, Kingston Brewster, Jr., another CFR member, and author of *Reflections on Our National Purpose*, as saying, "Our national purpose should be to abolish our nationality." Ward says, "The lust to surrender the sovereignty and independence of the United States is pervasive throughout most of the (CFR) membership."[9]

View from the Inside

Certainly the most revealing disclosure of the origins, aims and activities of the CFR came from one of their council's own members—Carroll Quigley, professor of history at the Foreign Service School of Georgetown University. His massive 1,300-page book, *Tragedy and Hope*, is an eye-opener. W. Cleon Skousen summarizes the volume in this way:

> When Dr. Quigley decided to write his 1,300 page book called *Tragedy and Hope*, he knew he was deliberately exposing one of the best kept secrets in the world. As one of the elite "insiders" he knew the scope of this power complex and he knew that its leaders hoped to eventually attain total global control. Furthermore, Dr. Quigley makes it clear throughout his book that by and large he warmly supports the goals and purposes of the "network." But if that is the case, why would he want to expose this worldwide conspiracy and disclose many of its most secret operations? . . .
>
> He says, in effect, that it is now too late for the little people to turn back the tide. In a spirit of kindness he is therefore urging them not to fight the noose which is already around their necks. He feels certain that those who do will only choke themselves to death. On the other hand, those who go along with the immense pressure which is beginning to be felt by all humanity will eventually find themselves in a man-made millennium of peace and prosperity. All through his book, Dr. Quigley assures us that we can trust these benevolent,

well-meaning men who are secretly operating behind the scenes. They are the hope of the world. All who resist them represent tragedy. Hence, the title for his book.[10]

Especially telling is Quigley's own assessment of the "conspiracy" in an oft-quoted passage from his book:

There does exist, and has existed for a generation, an international Anglophile network which operates, to some extent, in the way the radical Right believes the Communists act. In fact, this network, which we may identify as the Round Table Groups, has no aversion to cooperating with the Communists, or any other groups, and frequently does so. I know of the operations of this network because I have studied it for twenty years and was permitted for two years, in the early 1960's, to examine its papers and secret records. I have no aversion to it or to most of its aims and have, for much of my life, been close to it and to many of its instruments. I have objected, both in the past and recently, to a few of its policies . . . but in general my chief difference of opinion is that it wishes to remain unknown, and I believe its role in history is significant enough to be known.[11]

Sousken further reviews the content of *Tragedy and Hope*:

We learn from Professor Quigley that the conspiracy also has a British branch among whose instrumentalities is the Royal Institute of International Affairs. In the United States, the Institute "is known as the Council on Foreign Relations." A first purpose of the conspirators was to reunite the British Empire and United States under a single government which in effect would be a World Government.[12]

Master Conspiracy, another book by Quigley, was completed

48

in 1944 but went unpublished because no publisher could then be found who would handle it. It was released in the early 1980s. Commenting on Quigley's book in an article entitled "Proofs of a Conspiracy," Alan Stang writes:

> So immense, so awesome, is the power of this Conspiracy, that it even scares Quigley! He says of the Royal Institute of International Affairs: ". . . When the influence which the Institute wields is combined with that controlled by the Milner Group in other fields—in education, in administration, in newspapers and periodicals—a really terrifying picture begins to emerge. . . . The picture is terrifying because such power, whatever the goals at which it may be directed, is too much to be entrusted safely to any group. . . ."[13]

Alan Stang concludes his article with this summary:

> Bear in mind that we have cited but a few examples from Professor Quigley's books. Your intrepid correspondent could just as easily have written this piece with an entirely different set of examples. So we strongly urge you to obtain copies of these books and see for yourself.
>
> When you do, you will see even more undeniably than you do here that there is a Conspiracy. You will see, to a great extent, who is running it, including some of their names. Yes, names. Real names, composed of familiar letters! You will see how the Conspiracy operates and what it wants. You will see all this couched in a wealth of scholarly footnotes and references that you can and should check for yourself.
>
> When you have finished, you will realize that any conclusion that there is no Conspiracy out to rule the world is simply asinine. Indeed, it is insidious.[14]

Bearing out Quigley's claims, the CFR in one of their own

publications has advocated "building a new international order . . . responsive to world aspirations for peace, for social
and economic change . . . an international order including
states labeling themselves as socialist."[15]

It does appear as though a conspiracy could exist.

Shades of Orwell's 1984!

The question, however, as suggested before, is whether the
current serious global economic conditions (described in Chapter 2 and earlier in this chapter) have been created by the
Trilateralists in their efforts to achieve control, or whether the
world economy is now totally out of anyone's control!

Opinions vary. Some, like Gary Allen, feel things are virtually out of control. He says:

> In these complex times there are more strings than
> any single group of men could possibly control. While
> it is probably true that our Establishment Insiders have
> in the past created wars and depressions for their own
> benefit, these things happened in the days when such
> trauma could be somewhat localized. Given today's "in-
> terdependent" global economy, it is no longer easy to
> keep a major crisis localized. Everything affects every-
> thing else.
>
> . . . Which is why we believe the Insiders probably
> do not now wish to try to facilitate a major financial cri-
> sis. The probability of backfire is just too great. They
> want to prevent any kind of widespread panic or col-
> lapse. Even they must have sweaty palms. . . .
>
> . . . Nevertheless, there is always the X-Factor: some
> unforeseen watershed event or panic which can neither
> be planned for nor controlled.[16]

Others feel the current conditions have been planned.
Wally Woods, Jr., author of *Cashless Society: A World Without
Money* and publisher of two monthly newsletters of news

analysis, believes the chaos is by design. In an article entitled "New Money for a New World," he says:

> Space does not allow us to go into much detail at this time. We will say, however, that our present system of economics is on the precipice of total collapse. The depression that is just ahead promises to be more overwhelming than the one in the thirties. It will not, however, be an 'accidental' depression—it will occur by design. Its purpose will be to bring the world, especially the United States, to its knees, crying out for something—or, someone—to change things around to alleviate the pain.
>
> That "something" will be a new world order . . . that "someone" will be the new world leader of inestimable charisma and power. And the whole world will be deceived.[17]

But whether the present instability is by design or by accident really doesn't matter.

The effect is the same.

When the economic fabric of a society is torn apart, that society begins to disintegrate. The resulting confusion is the kind of environment in which an elite group— or a tyrant— can gain control. John Maynard Keynes has written:

> Lenin was certainly right. There is no subtler, no surer means of overturning the basis of existing society than to debauch the currency. This process engages all the hidden forces of economic law on the side of destruction, *and does it in a manner not one man in a million is able to diagnose.* [emphasis mine][18]

And whether the Trilateralists and their elitist cohorts planned the current economic uncertainty or if it is simply a matter of circumstances playing into their hands, Hal Lindsey makes a valid point when he says that the Trilateralist movement is unwittingly setting the stage for the political-economic one-world system the Bible predicts for the last days. It's happening in concert with all the other pieces of the prophetic scenario falling into place.

What the Trilateralists are trying to establish will soon be controlled by the coming world leader—the anti-Christ himself.[19]

Unquestionably, there will appear on the stage of human affairs a world-class economist who will offer solutions and controls that will capture the support (both willing and unwilling) of the world.

This economist-to-come, "Mr. 666" (who will have, I believe, a meteoric rise to power through the enabling of Satan), will become, in the truest sense of the word, a global dictator.

For behind the inexorable move toward a repressive one-world government that rules out God is Satan himself. He will use every means available to achieve this end, whether through witting or unwitting, willing or unwilling, benevolent or malevolent individuals and groups. He is the ultimate conspirator.

In the next chapter we'll take a look at what the ancient Scriptures have predicted about this coming global ruler who serves Satan's ends.

Notes

1 *Atlantic Monthly*, September 1975, pp. 28, 30.
2 H. Lindsey, op. cit., p. 124.
3 *U.S. News & World Report*, February 21, 1977, p. 34.
4 Ibid., p. 33.
5 H. Lindsey, op. cit., p. 125.
6 Ibid.
7 *"W" Magazine* (Fairchild Publications, 7 East 12th, New York, NY, 10002), August 4-11, 1978, p. 21.

8   H. Lindsey, op. cit., p. 127.

9   Ibid., p. 128.

10 W.C. Skousen, *The Naked Capitalist* (Salt Lake City: published privately, 1970), pp. 4-5.

11 C. Quigley, *Tragedy and Hope* (New York: MacMillan Company, 1966), pp. 136-144.

12 *American Opinion*, October 1982, p. 84.

13 Ibid., pp. 26, 81.

14 Ibid., p. 84.

15 *CRF Special Study, No. 7;* November 25, 1959.

16 *American Opinion*, November 1982, p. 94.

17 W. Wood, Jr., *New Money for a New World*, September 1981, p. 3.

18 As quoted in *The Coming Currency Collapse*, p. 21.

19 H. Lindsey, op. cit., p. 128.

"But you, Daniel, close up and seal the words
of the scroll until the time of the end."

—Angelic messenger to Daniel, the Prophet

CHAPTER 6

Tomorrow's News—from Dusty Writings!

Those ancient Hebrew prophets were something else!
Drawn from various walks of life, ranging from a herds-
man to a prime minister, they boldly proclaimed that they
were speaking for God.

Their utterances touched on many aspects—their own nation and times, empires through the ages and the coming life,
death, burial, resurrection and ascension of Jesus Christ, to
note but a few. (For documentation of the Hebrew prophets'
authenticity and reliability, please see Appendix A.)

And what they had to say also relates to events which are
appearing in our news media today—as well as tomorrow's
headlines! For the prophets predicted that at the end of time
a one-world government, headed by earth's final dictator
who is described in Scripture as the Antichrist, would come
into existence.

This amazing individual will be energized and controlled
by Satan. He will have an incredible rise to power and will
quickly assume control over the peoples of earth. The pro-

phetic writings indicate that only those who acknowledge their allegiance to this dictator by taking his mark (either on their foreheads or their right hands) will be permitted to buy or sell. This means that he will exercise life or death power over earth's inhabitants.

Only a short while ago such a prospect was considered by the skeptics to be a virtual impossibility. Now, however, in the light of developments such as we touched upon in Chapter 3, that which seemed to be absolutely impossible is now very much an eventuality.

Let's look at the specific predictions to be found in the Word of God.

Daniel's Description

The Antichrist first appears in the prophecy of Daniel. Before we look at the specific prophecy about him, we need to have some background. In Daniel Chapter 2, Daniel is enabled by God to interpret Nebuchadnezzar's dream. The dream is about a great image with head of gold, chest and arms of silver, abdomen and thighs of brass, legs of iron and feet and toes of iron and clay mixed. A stone strikes the image on its feet, causing it to collapse, after which the stone begins to grow and fills the earth. The interpretation that the dream is about the future course of human affairs is given to Daniel by God in verses 36-45.

The Interpretation

The image represents empires. The golden head is Babylon, the silver chest, Medo-Persia; the bronze abdomen, Greece; the iron legs, Rome; and the feet and toes of iron and clay mixed, a ten-nation federation understood to be the revived Roman Empire.

Dr. John Wesley White, in *The Coming World Dictator*, quotes *The European Community Magazine*, official publication of the European Union, as saying, "The EC Rome treaty supports the interpretation of the Books of Ezekiel, Daniel and the Revelation that this 'last days' kingdom is a new Roman Empire."[1]

The stone represents the kingdom of God which is established eternally in the days of the ten-nation federation.

Another Perspective

Further insight is provided in a prophetic vision recorded in Daniel Chapter 7, where the same empires are symbolized by four strange beasts. The fourth beast, which like the feet and toes of iron and clay in the first vision, represents a revived Roman empire, had, in addition to iron teeth, ten horns:

> After that, in my vision at night I looked, and there before me was a fourth beast—terrifying and frightening and very powerful. It had large iron teeth; it crushed and devoured its victims and trampled underfoot whatever was left. It was different from all the former beasts, and it had ten horns. (7:7)

From these ten horns grew an additional "little horn" which uprooted three of the other horns and "made war with the saints" (7:8, 21, KJV). From this we understand that earth's coming final ruler arises out of the revived Roman Empire, probably from one of the lesser nations (a "little horn"). He subdues three of the other ten nations and becomes supreme over the ten. Daniel described this horn in detail:

> While I was thinking about the horns, there before me was another horn, a little one, which came up among them; and three of the first horns were uprooted before it. This horn had eyes like the eyes of man and a mouth that spoke boastfully. . . .
>
> I also wanted to know about the ten horns on its head and about the other horn that came up, before which three of them fell—the horn that looked more imposing than the others and that had eyes and a mouth that spoke boastfully. As I watched, this horn was waging

war against the saints and defeating them, until the Ancient of Days came and pronounced judgment in favor of the saints of the Most High, and the time came when they possessed the kingdom.

He gave me this explanation: "The fourth beast is a fourth kingdom that will appear on earth. It will be different from all the other kingdoms and will devour the whole earth, trampling it down and crushing it. The ten horns are ten kings who will come from this kingdom. After them another king will arise, different from the earlier ones; he will subdue three kings. He will speak against the Most High and oppress his saints and try to change the set times and the laws. The saints will be handed over to him for a time, times and half a time." (7:8, 20-25)

Daniel tells us further that this little horn, the Antichrist, will make an agreement with Israel for one "week" of years (seven years) including the reestablishment of the ancient sacrifices, but in the middle of that agreement he will break it.

In Matthew 24:15 and 21, Jesus made reference to this and several other prophecies made by Daniel (Daniel 9:27, 12:11) concerning the future evil ruler. Here Christ spoke of "the abomination that causes desolation" which will cause sorrow unequaled in the history of the people of Israel.

He will confirm a covenant with many for one "seven." In the middle of the "seven" he will put an end to sacrifice and offering. And on a wing of the temple he will set up an abomination that causes desolation, until the end that is decreed is poured out on him. (9:27)

After breaking his agreement with Israel and the cessation of sacrifices, this diabolical king will exalt himself above every God, claiming that he himself is God and must be worshiped as God.

The king will do as he pleases. He will exalt and magnify himself above every god and will say unheard-of things against the God of gods. He will be successful until the time of wrath is completed, for what has been determined must take place. He will show no regard for the gods of his fathers or for the one desired by women, nor will he regard any god, but will exalt himself above them all. (11:36-37)

Further, he will be a man who honors force, who will become a blasphemer against God, a persecutor of the saints of God and one who will adjust laws and times to his advantage.

Instead of them, he will honor a god of fortresses; a god unknown to his fathers he will honor with gold and silver, with precious stones and costly gifts. He will attack the mightiest fortresses with the help of a foreign god and will greatly honor those who acknowledge him. He will make them rulers over many people and will distribute the land at a price. (11:38-39)

Prophecy from Paul

A good deal more prophetic information about the Antichrist comes through the apostle Paul in his second letter to the Thessalonians. In Paul's first letter to the believers at Thessalonica, he had written about the Lord's return to earth to take both dead and living saints to Himself (1 Thessalonians 4:13-18). However, this wonderful message of hope had confused the Christians there, for in the light of the difficult times they were undergoing, many of them concluded that they had missed that return and were already in the "day of the Lord" (5:2)—the period of Great Tribulation.

Paul very quickly and forcefully set that straight by writing, "Don't let anyone deceive you in any way, for that day will not come until the rebellion occurs and the man of lawlessness is revealed, the man doomed to destruction" (2 Thessalonians 2:3).

Then he went on to describe that "man of lawlessness." This coming ruler will oppose God, seek to exalt himself above God and even declare that he is God. To do so, the man of lawlessness will take his place in the temple and outlaw any worship not directed to him. He will be empowered by Satan to perform all kinds of counterfeit miracles, signs and wonders, deceiving those who are destined to perish because they refuse God's truth in order to be saved (2 Thessalonians 2:1-2).

The entire personality and mission of the Antichrist will be characterized by rebellion against God. The Greek word translated "falling away" (KJV) in 2:3 is *apostasia*, which can also mean "rebellion" or "revolt."

Now, it is true that, since the fall of mankind back in the Garden of Eden, humanity apart from Jesus Christ has been in a state of rebellion against God. This secret power of lawlessness, says Paul, "is already at work" (2:7). In and under the Antichrist, however, that rebellion will blossom into a deliberate, defiant, generalized, all-encompassing rejection of God and Christ. In the meantime, it is being restrained or held back by "he who now restrains" (2:7, NKJV).

I believe the restrainer is the Holy Spirit in the midst of His people, the Church (that body of believers all around the world in whom He dwells). In that sense, the Holy Spirit will be removed when Jesus snatches the Church away. This does not mean that the Holy Spirit will be absent from the earth. No, He will be present as He was during the Old Testament period before the birth of the Church. But, in His restraining-of-evil work in and through the Church, He will be removed at the Rapture (snatching away of believers).

And then the rebellion will spread rapidly until it is full-blown under the Antichrist, who will be its embodiment.

John Writes

Finally, John, in one of his letters and in the Revelation,

adds several more details on this coming evil one. In First John 2:18-27, he refers to the Antichrist. The Greek prefix translated "anti" has two meanings. One of these is "against" and the other "instead of." The Antichrist is not just against Christ but plans to be instead of Him.

Revelation describes the Apocalypse—the coming of Christ to this earth. The judgments of God upon the earth will be detailed in a scroll with seven seals, each seal containing judgments. When the seventh seal is opened, seven trumpets are blown, each marking a further judgment upon the earth. In turn, the seventh trumpet will introduce the seven vials or bowls judgments, the worst part of the Tribulation.

In that context, John prophetically describes the Antichrist and his counterfeit of the Holy Spirit, the evil False Prophet (Revelation 13). The nefarious activity, final struggle and doom of these evil personages is foretold in Revelation 19:11-21.

The Antichrist will be awesome. He will be empowered by Satan. He will blaspheme God. He will apparently rise from the dead or at least from what would be considered a fatal wound. He will take control of the world through unprecedented political authority and will be worshiped by all except the saints of God. He will appear to be invincible.

While the Antichrist will obviously handle political matters, his cohort, the False Prophet, will be in charge of religious affairs. It will evidently be a very religious time in which the False Prophet will perform miracles to win people to the worship of the dictator. One miracle will involve causing the statue of the Antichrist to apparently come to life (13:14-15).

Failing persuasion, there will be economic coercion—no one will be permitted to buy or sell unless he or she receives the mark of the Antichrist on forehead or hand. John declares that the mark is a number—666 (13:16-18).

Few portions of Scripture have triggered more speculation since, in Hebrew and Greek, each letter has a numerical value. Intriguingly enough, the total of those values in the

Antichrist's name comes to 666. All kinds of formulas have been unsuccessfully used through the years to "prove" that this person or that is the Antichrist.

John goes on to describe how God's wrath will be poured out on all who receive the beast's mark. In response, the arrogant, satanic Antichrist will rise against God and seek to destroy God's people, especially 144,000 Jews who (according to Revelation 7:1-8) have been sealed by God to bear witness to Him. Their divine seal will preserve them for this work from both the animosity of the Antichrist and the judgments of God's wrath.

This time period will culminate with the gathering to Jerusalem of armies from all the nations to fight God and the people of God, Israel. This will be the battle of Armageddon (14:14-20; 16:13-16).

The sequel to this fearful conflict will be the revelation of the Lord Jesus Christ and His armies from heaven. The Antichrist and his false prophet will be cast into the lake of fire (hell), and all of the rest of godless humanity slain (19:11-24).

How Soon?

I believe that earth's stage is being set for the enactment of these awesome events. And, though we know from Scripture that we are not to set dates, still anyone who reads the scriptural indicators—including potential economic collapse—must surely believe that the emergence of the end-time ruler is a distinct possibility.

In Chapter 5, we'll talk about why the setting of the stage will demand the appearance of this diabolical dictator—a fearsome wolf in sheep's clothing.

Note

1   As quoted in *The Coming World Dictator*, J.W. White (Minneapolis: Bethany Fellowship, 1981), p. 26.

*"And he causes all, both small and great, rich and poor,
free and bond, to receive a mark on their right hand,
or on their forehead, and that no one may buy or sell
except one who has the mark or the name of the beast, or the
number of his name. Here is wisdom. Let him that has
understanding count the number of the beast: for it is
the number of a man; and his number is six, six, six."*

—Prophet John on Patmos

CHAPTER 7

Setting the Stage for "Mr. 666"

As a child I had, as do most youngsters, a vivid imagination. Because I was the youngest by far of three siblings, and therefore like an only child, I had a good deal of opportunity to develop that imagination.

And since prophecy was a topic openly discussed in my home when a particular uncle came to visit, I had a lot of fuel for my creativity.

Uncle Fred was a prophecy buff. One of the areas of his interest was the predicted totalitarian control of the Antichrist—Mr. 666. Uncle Fred would wax eloquent in describing what he believed would be the horrors of that reign, little realizing, I'm sure, the impact such discussions were having on me as I sat and listened intently.

As I look back now, I understand where he was coming

from, for he had known personally what government oppression was, having come to Canada from Russia as a youth.

One of Uncle Fred's contentions was that the Canadian Social Insurance System with its individual numbers, just then being introduced, was the equivalent of the mark of the Antichrist.

I can recall how at night I used to snuggle down under the bed covers imagining that I was in a cave hiding from soldiers who were after me because I did not have the mark. I certainly did not intend ever to take the mark. On that point I was firmly settled, though I understood the entire matter only very dimly.

Both my uncle and my father have since passed away. But today we are witnessing developments in the area of control, such as the ones discussed in Chapters 2 and 3, which would have boggled my uncle's mind.

We've seen the one-world drive accelerate even as we've seen global conditions, especially financial, worsen to the point of crisis.

It is very easy to believe that the economic power to control all buying and selling by biometric numbering could happen. Technologically, it would appear that complete control is now feasible.

Coming Control

It is obvious to anyone who has done even a limited amount of research into the matter that mankind is ripe—technologically, politically and economically—for total control.

Let's look at a few of the clear indicators that this statement is not simply wild-eyed paranoia but solemn fact. The evidence is so vast that it would be impossible in a volume such as this to do any more than present some of the most significant reasons for such an assessment.

1. *A Cashless Society*. Total economic control of a people would be difficult, if not virtually impossible, unless that society were cashless. Even though legislation has now been passed that enables bill-by-bill tracking of U.S. currency and identifies the recipient, the statement stands.

I can recall being challenged years ago by skeptics who scoffed at the idea that buying and selling, as predicted in the Bible, could be controlled. However, with the advent of our current technology, particularly e-money, no longer is anyone scoffing at this possibility. We appear to be rapidly moving toward a truly cashless society.

We have long been users of plastic cash. Now cyber exchange is the coming medium. Software which secures electronic transactions on the Internet has been developed and its use is increasing dramatically in spite of the fact that there can be no absolute guarantees of total security.

CNN correspondent Marsha Walton comments:

> As buying by computer catches on, the device could eventually be used to pay for everything from a pizza delivery to bailing a friend out of jail, and would be as much a part of the home computer as a floppy disk or hard drive. And just as consumers have grown accustomed to computers and ATM cards, the combination of the two would be another step toward a "cashless society."[1]

TIME magazine reported:

> The push for a cashless society is gaining momentum, however, if only because making money disappear is also a way of saving money. There are about 12 billion pieces of U.S. paper currency, worth $150 billion, circulating worldwide, which works out to about $30 for every person on earth. Keeping all that paper in use is a costly chore for the government. Most $1 bills wear out after about 18 months. To retire, destroy and re-

place all aging currency costs the government an estimated $200 million a year. Currency is cumbersome for business as well. People have to count it, armored cars have to carry it, bank vaults have to store it and security guards have to protect it.[2]

David Warwick in *The Futurist* magazine extolled "The Cashless Society" in these words:

> The immediate benefits would be profound and fundamental. Theft of cash would become impossible. Bank robberies and cash-register robberies would simply cease to occur. Attacks on shopkeepers, taxi drivers and cashiers would all end. Purse snatchings would become a thing of the past. Urban streets would become safer. Retail shops in once-dangerous areas could operate in safety. Security costs and insurance rates would fall. Property values would rise. Neighborhoods would improve.
>
> Drug traffickers and their clients, burglars and receivers of stolen property, arsonists for hire, and bribe-takers would no longer have the advantage of using untraceable currency. . . . Sales of illegal drugs, along with the concomitant violent crime, should diminish. Hospital emergency rooms would become less crowded. Burglary statistics would fall.[3]

While the foregoing is viewed as being too optimistic, opinions vary, disadvantages are numerous and many oppose the concept, it is nonetheless apparent that the move is toward a truly cashless society. The distance we have come toward its implementation since it was first envisioned is mind-boggling.

On the downside, in terms of individual privacy, Stephen Levy in his article "E-money (That's What I Want)" warns: "Cyberspace cash systems in which 'every move you make and every file you take will be traceable' will open the door to surveillance like we've never seen."[4]

Having noted the above, however, it is only appropriate to observe that, as one banking expert put it, "we're not there yet and won't be for a long time." But even he qualifies this comment by stating that "long time" is a relative term. Also, given the current rapidity of change and technological advance, cashlessness could be a fact very soon.

2. *National ID*. Proposals for a government-controlled national identification (ID) system in the U.S. have been seriously put forward on numerous occasions. Invariably, such proposals have been turned aside by groups deeply concerned about the loss of individual privacy.

Recently a major effort to achieve such a national ID (though not identified as such) was made by the Clinton administration during its ill-fated drive to implement a universal health-care service in the U.S.

Called "a high-tech national tattoo" by Martin Anderson, a former Reagan aide who is now a Senior Fellow at the Hoover Research Institute at Sanford University in Palo Alto, California, the proposed health security card was further described as "an ingenuous device for keeping track of the personal lives of Americans."

The card was envisioned as a method of cracking down on welfare fraud, tracing deadbeat dads, supplanting Social Security cards, draft cards and passports—even registering voters and controlling voter fraud.[5]

The health-care proposal was defeated and the health security card, of course, never materialized. According to Anthony Sutton, author of *The Secret Establishment*,

> The defeat [of the health scheme] was a bitter pill for the Clintons—particularly since already signed Executive Orders to force the cards into use had apparently been made. *PC Week* asked the White House about [the orders] and was brushed off with "No comment."[6]

Nevertheless, the desire for a universal ID smart card is apparently alive and well.

One Clinton advisor who promoted the biochip "mark" is Dr. Mary Jane England, a member of the ill-fated national health-care initiative. Addressing a conference sponsored by computer giant IBM in Palm Springs, California, in 1994, England not only endorsed the proposed mandatory national ID Smart Card, but went a giant step further. As reported in *The New American*, July 25, 1995, she said:

> The smart card is a wonderful idea, but even better would be the capacity not to have a card, and I call it "a chip in your ear," that would actually access your medical records, so that no matter where you were, even if you came into an emergency room unconscious, we would have some capacity to access that medical record. We need to go beyond the narrow conceptualization of the smart card and really use some of the technology that's out there."[7]

The idea of microchips or miniature transponders being implanted into people is not at all farfetched. It's a well-established fact that such devices have already routinely been implanted in pets and other animals. And numerous published reports claim that many in the military carry electronic dog tags, some implanted. The widespread use of pacemakers demonstrates that the implantation of technological devices in the human body is no big deal.

A recent *Media Bypass* article stated:

> Implant technology is not new. Although routinely ridiculed by some as a paranoid delusion, the Food and Drug Administration (FDA) has mandated electronic biochip implants into humans receiving pacemakers, prosthetic devices, and even breast implants since 1994. Literally thousands of Americans now carry these micro devices under their skin. . . . Endangered animals

and livestock also carry implants to track their migration or feeding habits.[8]

In many ways an implanted personal information chip makes sense. It can't get lost or be stolen. It will require no maintenance. It would enable identification and care in the event of accident or illness in which consciousness is lost. The list of benefits is extensive. Consequently, entities other than government are, in fact, proposing such devices. An article by *Colorado Christian News* editor Joann Bruso pinpoints one such proposal:

> We knew it was coming. We've been talking about it for years. We've debated what it would look like, how it would be sold and implemented. Yet, somehow, it seems too soon. Last month while in Arizona, Andrew, my son-in-law, saw a very interesting commercial. Just before going to press, this same commercial was being aired in Colorado.
>
> In it a woman is pictured in an empty white room. As sets of numbers whiz by her head you hear them being read: social security, checking account, credit card, driver's license, health policy, telephone, fax, etc., etc.
>
> A voice asks, "How can you remember them all?" Then it declares, "MasterCard is working on the solution. The one-digit PIN (Personal Identification Number)."
>
> The camera then focuses on the back of the woman's right hand: she turns it over and you see a close-up of her index finger on which there is a pattern of dots. The voice-over states, "Your personal mark." It then proudly announces, "MasterCard will bring this benefit to you in the future!"
>
> Wow, what a marketing strategy! A new mark solving the problem of remembering all those numbers. Lost or stolen cards become a problem of the past. Just

scan your finger and, instantly, vital information is decoded.[9]

It does appear that, to an extent far greater than merely inclusive credit information, U.S. Social Security or Canadian Social Insurance Numbers, we are moving toward total ID. The pieces are all available.

3. *ISO9000—Business Control.* Though little known by people not involved in business or manufacturing, ISO certification is a significant and recent development on the world scene. In fact, it is possible that by or about the year 2000 no one on the planet, whether a company or an individual, will be able to make or sell products without international ISO9000 approval and certification. Already many nations have adopted the ISO standards as their own for quality control systems.

The ISO9000 website (http://www.bawtech.com.au/iso9000.htm) indicates that the certification applies to industries involved in the design and development, manufacturing, installation and servicing of products or services. The standards apply uniformly to companies in any industry of any size. ISO9000 is rapidly being universally accepted as the international standard.

ISO9000 certification began in Europe and at first was voluntary. By the end of 1999, however, it is scheduled to become mandatory. And ISO9000 is rapidly becoming the sole requirement for conducting commerce in all nations of the world. The statement of Sue Jackson, of Dupont Corporation's Quality Management and Technology Center, is typical: "ISO9000 is the quality system certification that companies, whether they be mills or suppliers, will need to have if they are to do business in a unified Europe, the U.S. and worldwide."

Rudolph G. Boznak, with the international consulting firm of United Research, Inc., writing in *Industrial Engineering* magazine, describes an international computer manufacturer who "painfully discovered that, because of ISO9000, $1.5 billion of his European sales were at risk. This corporation was told: Obtain ISO9000 certification for your products, or you're out!"[10]

A display ad published during 1991 by the Intertek Company proclaimed "With Intertek, You Won't Be Rejected on Seven Continents." The ad made the claim on the basis that the company was one of the first in the United States to have ISO9000 certification traceable to a European Union member country, noting also that ". . . more and more countries are enforcing these rigorous standards so our ISO9000 certification will be increasingly essential for anyone who sells abroad."

Quality magazine, a source of industrial information, reports that the National Accreditation Council for Certification Bodies, a London-based group (strangely enough), is "the official approving authority for third party registration boards in the United States."

Two American groups—The American Society of Quality Control and the American National Standards Institute—have also been given authority to "accredit registry board authorities throughout the U.S."[11]

The move to global ISO certification is on. During a speaking engagement in a small community near Pittsburgh, Pennsylvania in early 1998, I mentioned ISO9000 and asked if anyone in the audience was involved in manufacturing and was aware of the requirements. An employee of a small firm confirmed that they were being required, at substantial cost, to obtain ISO9000 certification.

While certification of quality control is commendable, the international aspect of such certification, originating in the European Union, does raise the specter of control in the hands of a small elite.

4. *L.U.C.I.D.*© *System.* An article in the September/October 1995 issue of *The Narc Officer* magazine provides information

on a startling concept dubbed L.U.C.I.D.© System which is being proposed with the intention of facilitating "Universal Computerized ID." The article contained a rather disturbing chart which depicted how the system would work.

The chart shows a family who represent Individual Universal Biometrics Cardholders. (The term "biometrics" refers to identification by human characteristics.) The individual members of the family are linked to the Universal Computerized Identification Clearinghouse Resource Center.

The Center, in turn, is shown to be the heart of the system with links to the legislative and executive branches of government, the National Criminal Justice System Telecommunication Services, the Criminal Justice System and the International Criminal Justice System Telecommunication Services—all connected to the L.U.C.I.D.© System Automated Data Processing.

The Biometrics Card, to be assigned to every individual, will contain templates, or samples, of the "individual's DNA genotype" and "his or her human leukocyte antigen." It will also contain profile and facial photos, fingerprints, footprints and iris scans of the eye. The technology to obtain such biometrics already exists. This Biometrics Card is also envisioned as having the capability to monitor bank accounts, purchases, transactions—in fact, all of the details of life.

The authors of L.U.C.I.D.© indicate that the system will be "an all-source fusion information center that will interface multilingual messages into a common communications network." This means that government, banking, educational, health, purchasing, business, military, etc., sources will be tapped. Messages from around the globe, in whatever language, will be collected and processed. It will be the single point, the global command center, for the surveillance of every person on earth.[12]

A good case can be made for such a system, given the threat of international nuclear and/or biological terrorism. In fact, the impetus for L.U.C.I.D.© was the Counter-Terrorism Act of 1995. L.U.C.I.D.© would also be a powerful weapon in the war on drugs, which explains the involvement of the Narcotics Department.

Nevertheless, it is easy to see how such a system, when fully implemented, could effect total control of all people. Additional extensive documentation of such control, though available, is beyond the scope of this volume.

Executive Orders and the Like

"But," you say, "people will never allow themselves to be so controlled."

Don't be so sure.

A little-known fact is that in the U.S. there are already a number of national security laws under the Emergency Powers Act which would allow the President, without further reference to Congress, an almost unbelievable degree of control.

A partial list of these already-enacted Executive Order laws includes:

- 10995 Seizure of all print and electronic communications media in the United States.

- 10997 Seizure of all electric power, fuels and minerals, public and private.

- 10998 Seizure of food supplies and resources, public and private, including farms and equipment.

- 10999 Seizure of all means of transportation, including cars, trucks or any other vehicles, including control over highways, harbors and waterways.

- 11000 Seizure of all American people for work forces under federal supervision; it allows the government to split up families if they deem it necessary.

- 11001 Seizure of all health, education and welfare facilities, public and private.

73

- 11002 Registration by the Postmaster General of all men, women and children for government service.

- 11003 Seizure of all airports and aircraft.

- 11004 Seizure of all housing and finance authorities; authority to establish forced relocation and to designate areas that must be abandoned as "unsafe." Establishment of new locations for population groups, building of new housing on public land.

- 11005 Seizure of all railroads, inland waterways and storage warehouses, public and private.

- 110051 Authorization for the Office of Emergency Planning to put the above orders into effect in times of increased international tension or financial crisis.

Grant Jeffrey, in *Final Warning*, comments:

Please note that these powers can be legally invoked by the president alone whenever he feels there is a time of increased tension or financial crisis. Every western democracy has similar laws which have been set up to provide for the continuity of government in the event of a major disruption such as a nuclear war. In both Canada and the United Kingdom, these laws are called Orders in Council and have been passed quietly by the Privy Council under the authority of the prime minister.[13]

Some observers feel that Y2K, the feared global disruption caused by widespread computer failure, could be the catalyst, not only in the United States, but around the world, to trigger the invoking of emergency powers.

There is a wide range of viewpoints on the potential effect of Y2K. While no one knows for sure what will happen, our consideration of why many fear its effect is worthy of our attention. It's our subject in Chapter 8.

Notes

1 Marsha Walton, "New Security Device to Broaden Business on the Web." Cable Network News Home Page, January 16, 1996, from the Internet.

2 Thomas McCarroll, "No Checks, No Cash, No Fuss?" *TIME*, May 4, 1994, Vol. 143, from the Internet.

3 David Warwick, "The Cash-Free Society," *The Futurist*, November-December 1992, p. 19.

4 Stephen Levy, "E-money (That's What I Want)," unpublished paper (1996), p. 2, from the Internet as quoted by Thomas Ice and Timothy Demy in *The Coming Cashless Society*.

5 Martin Anderson, *The Washington Times*, October 11, 1993, p. 3.

6 Anthony Sutton, "Why Clinton Wants Universal Health Care," *Phoenix Letter*, Vol. 13, No. 10, October 1994.

7 As quoted in *Project L.U.C.I.D.* (Austin, TX: Living Truth Publishers, 1996), pp. 115-116.

8 "Paranoid Reality: Doctors Implant Human 'Biochip'," *Media Bypass*, June 1996, p. 29.

9 Joann Chiarelo Bruso, "Big Brother Is Here," *Colorado Christian News*, March 1996, p. 8.

10 As quoted by Jackie Cox in "Is Mastering the Confusion of ISO9000 the Key to the Marketplace?" *American Papermaker*, June 1992, p. 1.

11 As cited in *Project L.U.C.I.D.*, pp. 132-136.

12 "L.U.C.I.D.© and the Counter-Terrorism Act of 1995," *The Narc Officer*, September/October, 1995, pp. 54-61, quoted in *Project L.U.C.I.D.*

13 Grant Jeffrey, *The Final Warning* (Eugene, OR: Harvest House Publishers, 1996), p. 136; John Loeffler, *Personal Update* (Koinea House, March 1998), pp. 8-11.

Failure to achieve compliance with Year 2000 will jeopardize our way of living on this planet for some time to come.

—Arthur Gross, Assistant IRS Commissioner

CHAPTER 8

The Y2K Bug: How Badly Will It Bite?

There is, of course, a very wide range of opinions on the seriousness of Y2K's effect on society.

The millennium bug (Y2K for short), as is widely known by now, is the fearfully anticipated computer problem. It has been created by the fact that the vast majority of computerized functions throughout the world, unless they are of recent design or have been made compliant, are based on the two digit expression for the date, i.e., 99 for 1999.

The difficulty, which will kick in on January 1, 2000, is that 00 will be read by all noncompliant mainframes, computers and microchips as 1900. The result may be serious malfunctions, lockups and shutdowns.

Predictions on what could happen range all the way from denials of any major problem through to forecasts of a total meltdown of the global economy and human society.

On the scary end of the scale, authors like Edward Yourdon (*Time Bomb 2000*), Michael Hyatt (*The Millennium Bug*) and Grant Jeffrey (*The Millennium Meltdown*) sketch potential scenarios that are positively frightening. For example, Hyatt paints the following partial picture of what could happen:

- Social Security checks will stop coming.

- Planes all over the world will be grounded.

- Credit card charges will be rejected.

- Military defense systems will fail.

- Police records and emergency communications will be inaccessible.

- There will be massive, long-term power failures.

- Bank funds will be inaccessible.

- Insurance policies will appear to have expired.

- Telephone systems will fail to operate.

- IRS tax records and government funds will be unavailable.

- The Federal Reserve System will be unable to clear checks.

- Time security vaults will fail to open or close on time.

- Traffic signals will fail to function.

- Office systems will fail and your employer will go out of business.

- There will be food shortages.

- Water and sewage disposal systems will not operate.[1]

He outlines five of the serious problems which could occur in a worst-case scenario in the banking system.

1. *Loss of faith by the public in the banking system.* As indicated in Chapter 3, if there is one thing that holds the entire current fiat money system together it is confidence. If that is

lost, one result could be a "bank run." If enough people with-draw their cash, the demand will exceed the bank's supply, a situation which could spread rapidly.

The trigger that could set this kind of collapse in motion could be either the fact that the banks are not Y2K-compliant or the *belief* that they are not. Hyatt quotes the testimony be-fore Congress of Jeff Jinnett, a Y2K expert, who said:

> . . . even if almost all of the U.S. financial institutions become fully Year 2000 compliant, a highly publicized computer system failure in one institution, together with the resulting litigation, may prompt stock market analysts and investors to "short" the stocks of other companies in the affected business sector. . . . [Also,] depositors may become concerned about their ability to access their funds if a "run" on their bank ultimately oc-curs. "Doomsday" articles alleging that federal govern-ment agencies and/or state agencies are unlikely to become Y2K compliant may add "fuel" to the flames.[2]

2. *Rise in security problems as a result of hackers taking advan-tage of Y2K disruptions.* Hyatt cites the statement of William J. McDonough, president of the Federal Reserve Bank of New York:

> Security also is likely to be of increasing concern. As [Y2K] time pressures mount, there is a risk that short-cuts will be taken. The checking of credentials for new staff or outside consultants or contractors may be rushed and less vigorous. Date-dependent security ap-plications may be turned off to facilitate testing.[3]

Consequently, the situation could give outside access to a financial institution's most sensitive data—its customers' per-sonal records—a scenario made to order for hackers who seek to gain unauthorized entry to financial systems' databases.

3. *Increase in bad debt from businesses that fail and are unable to repay their loans.*

4. *Increase in litigation stemming from Y2K problems.* Experts estimate that Y2K-related litigation, worldwide, could exceed $1 trillion.

5. *Possibility that many of the above losses won't be insured.*

This short and incomplete overview of some of the potential problems does not begin to examine the many other areas of major concern, including the fact that a U.S. Y2K-induced banking failure would mean the collapse of the U.S. economy—the final domino preventing a global economic meltdown.

It Can Be Fixed—Right?

Wrong—at least according to many computer experts. The reason given is that an incredible number of mainframes, personal computers and embedded microchips throughout the world are noncompliant as of late 1998.

They *can* be made compliant or replaced. It isn't a case of not knowing what to do. But doing what must be done is a technical, time-consuming, expensive process.

Unfortunately, according to many experts, the world is running out of both time and programmers who can fix the problem. To add to the critical nature of the dilemma, many of the old systems have encoded chips which were programmed in computer languages (like COBOL or FORTRAN) that are no longer in use, by programmers who are either retired or dead.

And there are millions upon millions of chips, to say nothing of mainframes and PCs, which need to be made compliant. For example, Hyatt reports:

> As it turns out, government agencies and large corporations all have millions of lines of code to review and repair. The U.S. Department of Defense (DoD) has as many as one billion lines. AT&T has five hundred million lines. The IRS has over one hundred million lines.

The SSA has over thirty million. The nation's two largest banks—Chase Manhattan and Citicorp—together have more than six hundred million lines.

To put this into perspective, the SSA (Social Security Administration) started correcting its Y2K problem relatively early. In 1991 the SSA assigned four hundred full-time programmers to the project. By mid-1996, after five years of steady work, they had reviewed and repaired six million lines of code— only 20 percent of the total! The Gartner Group, which is arguably the most respected and highly quoted Y2K research company in the world, estimates that half of all businesses are going to fall short. They also estimate that half of all government agencies [in the U.S.] are not going to make it.[4]

Grant Jeffrey adds some disconcerting details:

Arthur Gross, assistant IRS commissioner and key spokesman for the Internal Revenue Service, said: "The best estimate now is that the IRS has to plow through forty million lines of computer code and 30,000 applications." He later called the task "massive" and revised it to one hundred million lines and 50,000 applications, adding that "Failure to achieve compliance with Year 2000 will jeopardize our way of living on this planet for some time to come."

One of the most knowledgeable experts on the Year 2000 problem is Dr. Gary North, author of *The Remnant Review*. He has an excellent Web site on the Internet (http://garynorth.com) that compiles the latest information from government and industry on the state of the crisis. Dr. North reported in April 1998 that, to date, "no government tax collection agency above the county level is Year 2000 compliant today."[5]

The May, 1998, quarterly report of the House Committee monitoring the Federal government's readiness for Year 2000 revealed that only three of the sixteen major departments had an "A" grade on their progress to that point. Four had a "D" and five (including the crucial Department of Energy) had an "F." The overall government grade was a failing "F."[6]

To return to the domino illustration on the economy used by *Newsweek*, if the U.S. government cannot collect over one trillion in taxes, customs dues and the like, it will then be unable to pay its millions of civilian and military employees. Even if everything else in society is working well (a somewhat doubtful supposition), consider the effect on households, businesses and the economy if billions of dollars of salary income were suddenly unavailable.

Undoubtedly, the potential for Y2K to bring down the United States economy, the final national domino standing in the way of global meltdown, is very real.

In none of the above has consideration been given to the possible effect of paralyzed or badly hampered military and police forces; the potential of criminal activity in the cyberworld; the inability to supply consumers with food, water and waste disposal, particularly in the cities; the awesome danger of nuclear plants malfunctioning and creating "Three Mile Island" situations, or the breakdown of Internet, telephone, TV and radio communications, to mention only some of the major areas of possible difficulty.[7]

Neither has the state of unreadiness in most of the rest of the world been addressed. That's significant, since the fear is that compliant systems could be brought down by noncompliant ones as occurs with a virus. In fact, the Y2K problem has been dubbed "the Doomsday virus."

In Asia, Russia, Africa and Latin America and even Japan, government officials and corporations appear to be largely unaware of the threat. Consequently, financial centers in New York and London are reported to be already planning to cut off electronic computer communications with these nations January 1, 2000 to prevent their noncompliant systems from crashing those that are compliant.

We Could Be Hurtin'—or Maybe Not

Does the Y2K problem really have the potential to trigger chaotic global conditions?

Maybe. But maybe not.

Those who believe that the disruptions will be relatively minor could be right. In actual fact, however, nobody knows what will happen. If you should be reading this after January 1, 2000, and the disruptions have been minor, you will know that the prophets of doom were wrong. But, as one computer expert put it, "There are two kinds of people: those who aren't working on the problem and aren't worried, and those who are working on it, and are terrified." Peter de Jager, considered a leading Y2K expert in Canada, says that the people who aren't concerned are, for the most part, "outside the [computer] industry."[8]

The bottom line is that the danger signals which threaten the U.S. economy—inaccurate statistics, monetized debt, true inflation, galloping national debt, onerous tax burdens, Federal Reserve tinkering, potential stock market problems and banking crisis, all made potentially more serious by the specter of Y2K—clearly suggest that the outlook for the United States' and the world's economies is a bleak one.

And, if the worst happens, what then? Chaos would result if a global economic collapse should occur, created in part by and coupled with the Millennium 2000 problem.

Who can predict exactly what would happen in that eventuality? We do know that, as a fact of history, chaotic times have invariably produced dictators. Hitler was one of the more recent and most repugnant examples. Thus, in our global village, a global chaos could produce a global dictator. This is particularly plausible given the fact that there has been a pervasive one-world push underway in recent years. Such a ruler will have at his disposal the capacity to exercise life and death control through the medium of economics—the ability to buy and sell.

Politically, the one-world effort has been led by the United Nations. Religiously, the World Parliament of Religions and those behind it have been the driving force for a one-world situation. That we have arrived at a one-world economy is a fact that requires little proof.

One-world government. One-world religion. One-world economy. One-world leader. It appears that we're moving toward the imminent fulfillment of the ancient prophecies of the Bible.

Let's look next in detail at what the prophetic Scriptures have to say about the predicted future global ruler who will use the economy to assert and maintain his control.

Notes

1 Michael Hyatt, *The Millennium Bug, How to Survive the Coming Crisis* (Washington, DC: Regnery, 1998), back cover copy.

2 Ibid., p. 87.

3 Ibid., p. 88.

4 Ibid., pp. 11-12.

5 Grant Jeffrey, *The Millennium Meltdown* (Toronto, ON: Frontier Research Publications, Inc., 1998), pp. 129-131.

6 Information based on data prepared for Steven Horn, Chairman of the House Committee on Government Management, Information and Technology, February 15, 1998, as presented in *The Millennium Meltdown*.

7 For those who may be concerned about the possible effect of the millennium bug on them and/or on their family, a checklist of practical things which may be done to prepare for Y2K survival is provided in Appendix B.

8 Peter de Jager, *British Columbia Report*, February 23, 1998, p. 32.

"After them another king will arise. . . .
He will speak against the Most High and oppress his saints. . . .
He will try to change the set times and laws."

—Daniel, the Prophet

CHAPTER 9

His Infernal Majesty's Portrait

Years ago a short paragraph in a feature article in our local newspaper captured my attention, and I filed it away.

> Hyperinflation, I fear, can only pave the way to the abandonment of democracy and its replacement by dictatorship. Hitler and Napoleon both rode to power on the back of inflation.[1]

Today, that comment seems much more relevant than it did when I first read it. For according to the prophecies of Daniel, Jesus, Paul and John, as indicated in Chapter 5, such a man will come on the scene.

He will, after his initial settling-in period (which will include a treaty with Israel and the reestablishment of the ancient Jewish sacrifices in a restored temple), reveal his true diabolical and dictatorial nature. He will declare that he is god—and will demand that he be worshiped in the restored temple.

What Will He Look Like?

The composite picture of the Antichrist, obtained from the prophets, is not an attractive one, though it is most intriguing.

He is obviously a regal character. He is called *a stern-faced king* in Daniel 8:23; *the ruler who will come* in 9:26; and *the king [who] will do as he pleases* in 11:36. His self-will is amplified in Chapter 11 where he is characterized as rejecting all the traditional views of deity; he will *say unheard-of things against the God of gods*, verse 36; and will *show no regard for . . . one desired by women*, verse 37 (which is a reference to the desire of every devout Hebrew woman to be the mother of the Messiah).

Not only will he totally and blasphemously reject the traditional view of God, but he will worship the *god of forces* (KJV), verse 38. His confidence will be in military might.

Walter K. Price, in *The Coming AntiChrist*, presents an excellent, well-documented study of earth's final tyrant. In it he clearly demonstrates how the historical tyrant Antiochus IV Epiphanes is a type of the coming Antichrist and draws a number of parallels between the two.

From Scripture and the record of Antiochus, Price lists these characteristics of the Antichrist in addition to those we have already noted.

He will be a *persecutor of the Jews* (Daniel 12:1). He will *declare that he is god and demand worship* (2 Thessalonians 2:4). This will mean that he will *bring an end to the reinstituted Jewish sacrifices* (Daniel 9:27b), *place his image in the restored temple* (9:27, 12:11, Matthew 24:15, 2 Thessalonians 2:2-4) and *magnify himself as God* (Daniel 8:25, 11:36; 2 Thessalonians 2:4). He will *demand the death penalty for failure to worship* and will *regulate this by a mark* on people (Revelation 13:15-18). More about the future aspects of this worship shortly.

He is called *the man of lawlessness* (2 Thessalonians 2:2-4); *the man doomed to destruction* (2 Thessalonians 2:3); *the Antichrist* (1 John 2:18, 22, 4:3 and 2 John 7); *a beast* (Revelation 13:1) and *the lawless one* (2 Thessalonians 2:7-10).

Other Bible prophecies lead us to believe that the Antichrist may be killed (or apparently killed) and rise again. Three times in Revelation 13 (vs. 3, 12) it is said that the Beast suffers a "fatal wound [that] had been healed."

Whether this is an actual resurrection or an apparent one cannot be positively stated from the Scripture available. My personal view is that it is only apparent—since Satan does not have the power of life. But whether real or only apparent, it is obviously an effort to counterfeit the resurrection of Jesus Christ.

The Counterfeit Trinity

The counterfeit concept runs through all of this. The Antichrist is only one part of a counterfeit trinity—with Satan the counterfeit of God, Antichrist the counterfeit of the Lord Jesus Christ and the False Prophet the counterfeit of the Holy Spirit.

In Revelation 13, we see this evil trinity at work, for verse 2 says that "the dragon [Satan] gave the beast [Antichrist] his power and his throne [position], and great authority." Verse 4 makes it clear that worship of the Antichrist is really worship of Satan: "Men worshiped the dragon because he had given authority to the beast, and they also worshiped the beast. . . ."

Later in Revelation 13, the activities of the third person of the counterfeit trinity are described. Just as the Holy Spirit represents and magnifies Christ (John 16:13), so the False Prophet will promote the Antichrist:

> And he [the False Prophet] performed great and miraculous signs, even causing fire to come down from heaven to earth in full view of men.
>
> Because of the signs he was given power to do on behalf of the first beast, he deceived the inhabitants of the earth. He ordered them to set up an image in honor of the beast who was wounded by the sword and yet lived.
>
> He was given power to give breath to the image of the first beast, so that it could speak and cause all who re-

fused to worship the image to be killed. (Revelation 13:13-15)

Many have speculated that, at the time of the death wound, the Antichrist (who most certainly will be a man) will become totally possessed by Satan. He will become Satan incarnate. If so—and there is no good reason for refusing to believe this—it explains why worship of him will be, in fact, worship of Satan.

The tangible indication of that worship, according to Revelation 13:16-17, will be the receiving of a mark on either the right hand or the forehead—number 666!

> He also forced everyone, small and great, rich and poor, free and slave, to receive a mark on his right hand or on his forehead, so that no one could buy or sell unless he had the mark, which is the name of the beast or the number of his name.

Not so very long ago the skeptics had a field day with this one. They delighted in asking how it was going to be possible for anyone to exercise the kind of control which such a prophecy envisioned. However, as has been indicated in previous chapters, the technology that makes such control feasible now exists. When coupled with the one-world, one-religion emphasis, the parts seem to fit. As a result, knowledgeable folks no longer scoff at the idea of total control.

Thus, the ancient prophecies do appear to be coming to pass before our eyes.

The World Leader

Peter Lalonde, best-selling author, lecturer, broadcaster, researcher and coeditor of *This Week in Bible Prophecy*, some time ago analyzed what has been described as "The Blueprint for Building the New World Order."

In his article he details the various aspects of "The Blueprint." He lists these as: world government, piece-by-piece;

global management by crisis; critical instability as a factor, with the present economic system being shown to be at a point of critical instability; and transformation to world government through (1) social movements; (2) new science (which accepts the psychic human potential); the new image of man ("man is more than the sum of his mundane experiences: he is a spiritual entity, the ultimate reality is to be found in the realm of the spiritual and mystical, rather than the material and empirical"); and (3) a new central project for mankind (guided, as Willis Herman suggests, by the new image of man, i.e., a spiritual being with psychic potential).

At the apex of the blueprint is a world leader. Lalonde writes:

> Ervin Laszlo, of The United Nations Institute for Training and Research (UNITAR), in speaking of how all of the various crises—environmental, overpopulation, economic and political—combined with the new image of man, could bring about a moment of critical instability and thus a transformation to a New World Order, also noted another occurrence that will accompany the coming moment of critical instability:
>
> He said, "How does all this apply to the contemporary condition of humankind? The answer is, I believe, obvious. We are now about to enter an epoch of *critical instability*. Unlike past such epochs, it will *not be locally confined*. Our world is so strongly interdependent that an instability in any sector or any part can and will spread with great rapidity and destabilize all societies" [emphasis mine].
>
> Such new realities as high speed communication, instant worldwide media coverage and the political-economic interdependency of the world, according to Laszlo, means that any major crisis will be worldwide in scope and any solution will also have to be global. And likewise with regard to the leader who will be

thrust forward at this moment of critical instability, Laszlo concludes that he "will not be locally confined. He will become a worldwide leader." . . .

"What We Need Is a Man"

Historian Arnold Toynbee claims that "we are ripe for the deifying of any new Caesar who might succeed in giving the world unity and peace."

And as Henry Spaak, the former Secretary General of NATO, claimed as early as 1957: "We do not want another committee; we have too many already. What we want is a man of sufficient stature to hold the allegiance of all people and to lift us out of the economic morass into which we are sinking. Send us such a man and be he god or devil, we will receive him."

And much as the globalist leaders believe that the moment of critical instability will greatly amplify the call for a New World Order, they also believe that this "crisis of leadership" will be greatly magnified when a crisis or series of crises of unbelievable proportion hits the earth. It is in such a moment of crises that it seems that the Antichrist will emerge to fill this great leadership vacuum. And the Bible is very clear that the Antichrist will have great leadership capabilities . . . (Daniel 7:20; 7:8, 11; Revelation 13:5; Daniel 7:25; Revelation 13:8).[2]

Lalonde notes that it is not only the globalists who are looking for their "savior," but so are the Buddhists, the Muslims, the Hindus, the Jews and the New Agers. All expect their "savior" to come and set up the kingdom of God here on earth. All are wide open to the deception of the miracle-working Antichrist.

The secret to a managed crisis is to have people accept something as a resolution to the crisis that they would never have accepted if that "crisis" had not been brought to their attention. And when one begins to watch the highly publicized crises in the world today and the solutions being proposed to solve them, he begins to notice that in each instance the proposed solution is always a World Government, a World Court, World Law or a New International Economic Order— all parts of a New World Order.[3]

I feel quite certain that events like the Asian flu, Russian ruble meltdown and similar future upheavals are all important parts of the development of the "critical instability" which will create the one-world scenario in which the Antichrist will star.

Notes

1 Ronald Raeburn, *The Vancouver Sun*, April 3, 1980, p. A5.
2 Peter Lalonde, *The Omega Letter*, July-August 1987.
3 Ibid.

"And in the days of these kings shall the God of heaven set up a Kingdom which shall never be destroyed."
—Prophet Daniel in Babylon, about 600 B.C.

CHAPTER 10

Earth's Last Dictator

The early morning air was charged with tension that day in Nebuchadnezzar's court back about 600 B.C.

The king had had a dream the night before and now he wanted it to be interpreted for him. Accordingly, he called in all his court magicians, conjurors, sorcerers and Chaldeans so that they could tell him the meaning of his vision.

The only problem was that he had forgotten the dream even though it had made a tremendous impression upon him.

Nevertheless, he was insisting that his prognosticators tell him not only its meaning, but the forgotten dream as well!

Their frightened protests that this was unfair and unheard of produced a royal rage and the decree that, since they could not reveal both the dream and the interpretation, they should all be destroyed.

Before the mass execution could be carried out, however, Daniel, a captive Jew who had become prominent in Nebuchadnezzar's court as a wise man, made a promise to the captain of the guard that he would tell the king both the dream and its interpretation, if he were but given a little time.

A temporary reprieve was granted. Daniel and his three Hebrew friends gave themselves to prayer that God would reveal these secrets to him.

That night, God gave Daniel a vision.

He was hurried before Nebuchadnezzar and, after giving the credit for his knowledge to God, proceeded to tell the king what he had dreamed and what the dream meant. The revelation is one of the most significant prophecies ever uttered and explains why we say that the coming Antichrist will be earth's last dictator.

Before we look at the prophecy, a brief comment about Daniel.

Daniel—Man of Integrity

The authenticity of Daniel's prophecy has been repeatedly attacked over the years by many critics. In spite of the fact that both Jews and Christians accept the book of Daniel as part of the bona fide Old Testament Scriptures, the critics who do not accept the inspiration of Scripture claim that Daniel could not have written it. One of their main reasons is that the prophecies, as recorded especially in Chapter 11, give such an accurate picture of the future that the critics insist it has to be history, not prophecy. So they assert that Daniel was not written by Daniel and is dated about 165 B.C., instead of prior to 500 B.C.

There is ample evidence to defend both Daniel's authorship and the book's authenticity. Such defense is beyond the scope of this volume, and it has been admirably presented by others far better qualified than this author. A recent and notable apologetic is Josh McDowell's book, *Daniel in the Critics' Den*. You can count on it—Daniel's prophecy is bona fide. Jesus obviously believed Daniel to be genuine. In Matthew 24:15, He called him a prophet. So study Daniel's writings in complete confidence.

A Parade of Empires

Nebuchadnezzar's dream was of a great image, dazzling in its brightness and overpowering in its size and form. It had a head of gold, chest and arms of silver, abdomen and thighs of brass, legs of iron and feet of iron and clay mixed.

Then, in the dream, a stone was cut out without hands. It came and struck the image on its feet of iron and clay. The great statue collapsed, then disintegrated into dust which was blown away by the wind.

The stone which had caused the destruction of the statue then began to expand until it became a great mountain and filled all the earth.

We're not left to ponder what all of this means. The interpretation, as given by Daniel, is so significant that we should look carefully at exactly what Daniel said (2:36-43):

> This was the dream, and now we will interpret it to the king.
>
> You, O king, are the king of kings. The God of heaven has given you dominion and power and might and glory; in your hands he has placed mankind and the beasts of the field and the birds of the air. Wherever they live, he has made you ruler over them all. Thou art that head of gold.
>
> After you, another kingdom will rise, inferior to yours. Next, a third kingdom, one of bronze, will rule over the whole earth.
>
> Finally, there will be a fourth kingdom, strong as iron—for iron breaks and smashes everything—and as iron breaks things to pieces, so will it crush and break all the others.
>
> Just as you saw that the feet and toes were partly of baked clay and partly of iron, so this will be a divided kingdom; yet it will have some of the strength of iron in it, even as you saw iron mixed with clay.
>
> As the toes were partly iron and partly clay, so this

kingdom will be partly strong and partly brittle.

And just as you saw the iron mixed with baked clay, so the people will be a mixture and will not remain united, any more than iron mixes with clay.

In the time of those kings, the God of heaven will set up a kingdom that will never be destroyed, nor will it be left to another people. It will crush all those kingdoms and bring them to an end, but it will itself stand forever.

This is the meaning of the vision of the rock cut out of a mountain, but not by human hands—a rock that broke the iron, the bronze, the clay, the silver and the gold to pieces.

The great God has shown the king what will take place in the future. The dream is true and the interpretation is trustworthy. (Daniel 2:36-45)

Daniel told Nebuchadnezzar that the Babylonian empire, of which he was king, was the head of gold. The silver chest represented Medo-Persia; the bronze abdomen, Greece; the iron legs, Rome; and the feet and toes of iron and clay, a ten-nation confederacy. During the rule of this ten-nation entity, which arises out of the old Roman Empire, the God of heaven will establish His kingdom, which will have no end.

The coming of that kingdom will mark the culmination of all human rule, symbolized by the destruction, disintegration and sweeping away of everything that remains of the grand statue of human empires.

The coming Antichrist, who will reign over that final ten-nation empire, and through it, over the world, will be the last dictator which this poor old earth will see.

The world has witnessed a dreary parade of tyrants and dictators—some of the Pharaohs, the Assyrians, Roman emperors, Hitler, Stalin, Mao Tse-tung, Idi Amin and a host of lesser-known but nonetheless diabolical rulers.

Nothing which any of them has done, however, will equal

the incredible tyranny of the Antichrist. He will be the worst—and the last—dictator.

No more after him.

His defeat by God will usher in the reign of Christ, first in the Millennium and then eternally in the new heaven and earth.

In both Chapter 2 and Chapter 7 of Daniel's prophecy (parallel passages) we see how this future timetable is clearly presented.

Now, let's look a bit more closely at Daniel 7:19-25:

> Then I wanted to know the true meaning of the fourth beast, which was different from all the others and most terrifying, with its iron teeth and bronze claws—the beast that crushed and devoured its victims and trampled underfoot whatever was left.
>
> I also wanted to know about the ten horns on its head and about the other horn that came up, before which three of them fell—the horn that looked more imposing than the others and that had eyes and a mouth that spoke boastfully.
>
> As I watched, this horn was waging war against the saints and defeating them, until the Ancient of Days came and pronounced judgment in favor of the saints of the Most High, and the time came when they possessed the kingdom.
>
> He gave me this explanation: "The fourth beast is a fourth kingdom that will appear on earth. It will be different from all the other kingdoms and will devour the whole earth, trampling it down and crushing it.
>
> The ten horns are ten kings who will come from this kingdom. After them another king will arise, different from the earlier ones; he will subdue three kings.
>
> He will speak against the Most High and oppress his saints and try to change the set times and the laws. The

saints will be handed over to him for a time, times and half a time.

The message is clear.

In the days of a ten-nation political entity (the ten horns) which arises out of the old Roman Empire (the fourth beast), a diabolical world ruler will arise (the one predominant horn). He will be the final one, for in his reign the climax of earth's ages will occur and Christ's kingdom will be established.

How close are we to that time?

I believe very close.

In the preceding chapters we have attempted to document the powerful and accelerating drive for a one-world government. We've considered the economic crises which (if history teaches us anything at all) could precipitate the rise to power of any global strong man who can provide solutions. And we've looked at the technological advances which make possible the kind of totalitarian control the prophets envisioned.

We need to look in detail at what could well be that final ten-nation bloc, or at the very least, its forerunner—the European Union, previously known as the European Common Market.

Consider the European Union

That the Union (EU) may be Daniel's "ten-toed" or "ten-horned" kingdom is not at all far-fetched, as we will see.

The EU began in 1957 with the Treaty of Rome. Back then it was a six-member economic partnership. But even then it was envisioned as much more than that. Dr. Walter Hallstein, then president of the EU, described the vision:

> Three phases of the European unification are to be noted. First, the customs union, second, the economic union, third, the political union. . . . What we have created on the way to uniting Europe is a mighty economic-political union of which nothing may be sacrificed for any rea-

BABYLON
GOLD
626 - 538 B.C.

MEDO-PERSIA
SILVER
538 - 330 B.C.

GREECE
BRONZE
330 - 200 B.C.

ROME
IRON
200 B.C. - 500 A.D.

**TEN-NATION
CONFEDERACY (EU?)**
IRON & CLAY
1957 – ?

"In the days of *THESE KINGS* . . . the God of Heaven will establish His everlasting kingdom" (Daniel 2:44) [emphasis mine].

The prophesied empires

son. Its value exists not only in what it is, but more in what it promises to become. . . . At about 1980 we may fully expect the great fusion of all economic, military, and political communities together into the United States of Europe.[1]

Hallstein was inaccurate on the timing, but the direction and goal he described are right on target.

The six-nation partnership has become a fifteen-member entity which many observers believe not only will challenge the U.S. for world leadership but, in some ways, is already doing so.

Throughout its more than forty years of history, the European Union member nations have done, and are doing, a good deal of squabbling among themselves. Threats of withdrawal from the Union have not been infrequent. In many ways, like the iron and clay of the biblical image, the nations have not mixed well. Nevertheless, they have remained together and moved steadily toward a genuine union such as the one predicted by Hallstein.

Milestones along the road from being sovereign states which are merely cooperating together economically to the existence of a United States of Europe have included the creation of a common passport, a unified foreign affairs approach, customs union and the foreshadowing of a common currency, initially called the ecu.

An elected Parliament has functioned since the mid-1970s. A Council of Ministers and a Court of Justice are already permanent structures. In early 1998 a splendid new Parliament building was opened in the EU capital of Brussels, Belgium.

But nothing has even remotely equaled in importance the most recent milestone. In May, 1998, eleven of the fifteen EU nations agreed to fully unite economically in the European Monetary Union (EMU) beginning in 1999—a giant step toward surrender of individual national sovereignty. (The four EU members who either chose not to join, or were not yet qualified, are expected to enter within the next several years.)

The EU is huge. The fifteen member nations have within their borders over 370 million people, 10 million businesses and a gross domestic product (GDP) approaching $7 trillion, with a potential worth of $8.6 trillion.[2]

This makes it easily the largest economic entity in the world. By comparison, the U.S. economy, which is the largest single-nation economy in the world, has a GDP which is under $6 trillion.

When the new EU currency, to be called the euro, is launched, it is expected to challenge the U.S. dollar as the world's strongest currency. Norbert Walter, chief economist for Deutsche Bank, predicts: "The dollar and the euro are likely to wind up with about 40 percent of world finance each, with about 20 percent remaining for the yen and a few smaller currencies."[3]

Unquestionably, this union of nations arising out of the old Roman Empire is a big and powerful entity, poised, as one writer put it, for "a whole new era of growth." The capital of Brussels is now viewed as the "second Washington, DC" in terms of world power and influence—a situation which would have been considered absolutely preposterous fifty-plus years ago when World War II ended.

And it may get bigger, with numerous other nations from Eastern Europe and the Mediterranean wanting in. As many as twenty-five member nations are envisioned.

"Ten"—You Say?

So, if there are more than ten nations, the question arises as to how the EU could be the fulfillment of the ten-nation end-time confederacy.

It is a good question.

There are several possible answers.

The first is that the ongoing EU squabbles may result in a partial breakup, thus reducing the member nations to ten.

The European Union

Almost since day one of the Union, there have been disagreements and predictions of breakups. As recently as 1994, two of the major nations—Britain and Germany—threatened to pull out. Britain's then Prime Minister John Major once went to the very brink of political defeat over the issue of having Britain remain in the EU.

This instability fits the biblical symbolism—iron and clay do not mix well—and the feet and ten toes of iron and clay in Daniel's vision are an excellent representation of the shaky union of the EU throughout its history.

Another possible answer is that there could be a reversal of the idea of expansion coupled with a fallout as already indicated, bringing the EU number to ten.

An October 28, 1995, report in *The Economist* was headlined "The EU Goes Cold on Enlargement." The European Commission apparently concluded that the EU cannot afford to let into the union all those nations which have applied for entry. At least not for now.

A third, and, in my opinion, more plausible explanation is that of a concept already being considered by the EU. This recent idea is for the creation of a three-tier system within the union, a concept first publicly proposed by French Prime Minister Edouard Balladur in a speech on August 30, 1994.

Under the three-tier Europe being envisioned, the EU would be comprised of an "inner core of nations committed to full-blooded monetary, military and social union."

The concept has been fully endorsed by the German leadership, whose document *Reflections on European Policy* calls for such a systematic structure.

By late 1995, five of the EU member nations (Germany, France, Belgium, the Netherlands and Luxembourg) had agreed to relinquish their national sovereignty to an "inner core union." These nations, according to a September 8, 1994, report in *The European* newspaper, would seek to rapidly unite their countries into a transnational superstate with one currency, one army, one parliament and one foreign policy.

Balladur is quoted as saying, "[A] smaller number of EU member states must build an organization better structured, monetarily as well as militarily. Later we'll need to work to turn these three tiers into two, perhaps, much later into a single one." It has been suggested, however, that an inner core of ten nations may be the best solution to EU concerns.[4]

Another possible explanation is that the Antichrist is prophesied to "uproot" three of the nations (Daniel 7:8). Exactly what this means is not fully understood, except that it suggests turmoil and realignment.

In any event, this major development of the European Union appears to suggest that Christ's return could be near.

Economic Signs of Prophetic Fulfillment

Though inevitably interconnected with political, religious, social and technological developments, the economic indicators which we've considered in Part One are of supreme importance. In fact, they underlie all other signs—for truly "money [or its equivalent] is power."

The economy to come will demonstrate how that power is used by earth's last and most powerful human dictator.

Notes

1 Quoted in Hal Lindsey, *The Late, Great Planet Earth* (Grand Rapids: Zondervan, 1970), p. 85.
2 *Newsweek*, May 4, 1998, p. 42.
3 *The London Times*, May 12, 1998, p. A3.
4 *The Economist*, October 28, 1995, pp. 38-40.

PART TWO

The Climax of the Ages

Political Signs

Another of the indications that the world is moving into its predicted climax is the current alignment and activities of nations other than those of the European Union, particularly Israel.

Jesus indicated in His discourse on the Mount of Olives that the nation of Israel and the other nations of earth are likened to the fig tree and "all the trees," respectively.

Jesus said further that just as the person who sees leaves beginning to appear on the trees can know that summer is near, so the person who sees certain political signs appear can know that the climax of all human affairs is at hand.

In Part Two, we'll look at what I believe are current political events which qualify as "the bursting forth of the leaves."

"Summer" is near!

*"And in that day will I [the Lord] make
Jerusalem a burdensome stone for all people."*
—The Prophet Zechariah, writing about 487 B.C.

CHAPTER 11

Israel—A Problem to the Nations

The tiny nation of Israel—out of all proportion to its geo-graphical size and small population—for decades has been the world's chronic hot spot.

Although other global crises take priority from time to time, Israel has been most consistently the number one problem area. The average man on the street may not understand just why this is so, but the fact remains nonetheless.

For example, though little known, the world was pushed literally to the very brink of nuclear war at the time of the Yom Kippur War of 1973, as Lance Lambert carefully documents in his book, *Israel: A Secret Documentary*. Thus, any breakdown in the current ongoing efforts to find a peaceful solution to the conflict between the Israelis and Palestinians is viewed by world leaders as a potential threat to global peace.

That Israel even exists is nothing short of miraculous. To explain why, let's delve briefly into history, after which we'll indicate how the miracle of Israel's nationhood and survival is the key piece in the unfolding of the prophetic puzzle.

The Miracle of Israel's Birth

Israel as a nation has an amazing and unique history dating back nearly 6,000 years. The Bible describes how, in the beginning, God chose Abraham and promised to make of him a great nation. God also promised to give Abraham's children a land for their home. That land is clearly described in the Scriptures.

Later, in Egypt, where Abraham's descendants had gone to escape widespread famine, the family of Israel grew and became a nation. Subsequently, under Moses, they escaped what had become cruel bondage and finally, led by General Joshua, conquered Canaan which became their home—the land promised to them by God.

Along the way, they were given the Ten Commandments (see Exodus 20: 3-17) and the Pentateuch (the first five books of the Bible). God also made it very clear to the Israelites, through Moses, that if they obeyed the Word of God His blessing would be theirs. If they disobeyed, the judgments of the Almighty would be visited upon them. This agreement between God and His people is recorded in the Old Testament book of Deuteronomy:

Here's That Amazing Document

Blessing . . .

> If you fully obey the LORD your God and carefully follow all his commands I give you today, the LORD your God will set you high above all the nations on earth.
>
> All these blessings will come upon you and accompany you if you obey the LORD your God:
>
> > You will be blessed in the city and blessed in the country.
> > The fruit of your womb will be blessed, and the crops of your land and the young of your livestock—the calves of your herds and the lambs of your flocks.

Your basket and your kneading trough will be blessed.

You will be blessed when you come in and blessed when you go out.

The LORD will grant that the enemies who rise up against you will be defeated before you. They will come at you from one direction but flee from you in seven.

The LORD will send a blessing on your barns and on everything you put your hand to. The LORD your God will bless you in the land he is giving you. . . .

The LORD will open the heavens, the storehouse of his bounty, to send rain on your land in season and to bless all the work of your hands. You will lend to many nations but will borrow from none.

The LORD will make you the head, not the tail. If you pay attention to the commands of the LORD your God that I give you this day and carefully follow them, you will always be at the top, never at the bottom.

Do not turn aside from any of the commands I give you today, to the right or to the left, following other gods and serving them.

Judgment . . .

However, if you do not obey the LORD your God and do not carefully follow all his commands and decrees I am giving you today, all these curses will come upon you and overtake you:

You will be cursed in the city and cursed in the country.

Your basket and your kneading trough will be cursed.

The fruit of your womb will be cursed, and the crops of your land, and the calves of your herds and the lambs of your flocks.

You will be cursed when you come in and cursed when you go out.

The LORD will send on you curses, confusion and rebuke in everything you put your hand to, until you are destroyed and come to sudden ruin because of the evil you have done in forsaking him. . . .

The LORD will cause you to be defeated before your enemies. . . .

Your sons and daughters will be given to another nation, and you will wear out your eyes watching for them day after day, powerless to lift a hand. . . .

The LORD will drive you and the king you set over you to a nation unknown to you or your fathers. There you will worship other gods, gods of wood and stone. . . .

You will have sons and daughters but you will not keep them, because they will go into captivity. . . .

The LORD will bring a nation against you from far away, from the ends of the earth, like an eagle swooping down, a nation whose language you will not understand, a fierce-looking nation without respect for the old or pity for the young.

They will devour the young of your livestock and the crops of your land until you are destroyed. They will leave you no grain, new wine or oil, nor any calves of your herds or lambs of your flocks until you are ruined.

They will lay siege to all the cities throughout your land until the high fortified walls in which you trust fall down. They will besiege all the cities throughout the land the LORD your God is giving you. . . .

If you do not carefully follow all the words of this law, which are written in this book, and do not revere this glorious and awesome name—the LORD your God—the LORD will send fearful plagues on you and your descendants, harsh and prolonged disasters, and severe and lingering illnesses. . . .

You who were as numerous as the stars in the sky will be left but few in number, because you did not obey the LORD your God.

Just as it pleased the LORD to make you prosper and increase in number, so it will please him to ruin and destroy you. You will be uprooted from the land you are entering to possess.

Then the LORD will scatter you among all nations, from one end of the earth to the other. There you will worship other gods—gods of wood and stone, which neither you nor your fathers have known.

Among those nations you will find no repose, no resting place for the sole of your foot. There the LORD will give you an anxious mind, eyes weary with longing, and a despairing heart.

You will live in constant suspense, filled with dread both night and day, never sure of your life.

In the morning you will say, "If only it were evening!" and in the evening, "If only it were morning!"—because of the terror that will fill your hearts and the sights that your eyes will see. . . .

Covenant sealed . . .

These are the terms of the covenant the LORD commanded Moses to make with the Israelites in Moab, in addition to the covenant he had made with them at Horeb. (Selections from Deuteronomy 28:1–8, 12–20, 25a, 32, 36, 41, 49–52, 58–59, 62–67; 29:1)

The Tragic Cycle

History records the tragic story. Israel's national disobedience to God's laws, followed by His judgment, their repentance and God's promised aid, followed by disobedience, became a continuous cycle. The nation went steadily downhill spiritually and in every other way.

Finally, the chosen people were divided into two nations—the ten tribes of Israel to the north and the two tribes of Judah in the south. These two nations lived side by side for 200 years, often engaging in war between themselves as well as with the nations around them.

Meanwhile, their national disregard for God, worse in the ten northern tribes of Israel, continued and became so great that finally divine judgment permitted Israel's complete destruction as a nation. Her people were carried away into a captivity from which they would not return for centuries.

Judah, the southern nation, also experienced the judgment of God for its sin and was later conquered by a succession of enemies, though a remnant was permitted to remain in the land.

Later, under the Macabees, an independent Jewish state did exist for a brief time about 140 B.C. until the armies of Rome conquered all of the then-known world, including Judah.

During His earthly ministry, Jesus Christ, who lived in Israel and was crucified during the time of the Romans' dominion, added to the prophetic forecast on Israel. He said:

> When you see Jerusalem being surrounded by armies, you will know that its desolation is near.
>
> Then let those who are in Judea flee to the mountains, let those in the city get out, and let those in the country not enter the city.
>
> For this is the time of punishment in fulfillment of all that has been written. . . .
>
> They will fall by the sword and will be taken as prisoners to all the nations. Jerusalem will be trampled on by the Gentiles until the times of the Gentiles are fulfilled. (Luke 21:20–24)

That prophecy was literally fulfilled when, in A.D. 70, as a "final solution to the Jewish problem," the Roman general, Titus, brutally put down a rebellion, crucified hundreds of thousands of Jews, sold thousands more into slavery in other lands, razed the temple by fire and totally destroyed Jerusalem.[1]

A band of about 1,000 Jewish soldiers, women and children held out against the might of Rome for months in the desert stronghold of Masada, but when that heroic community finally fell in A.D. 100, the nation of Israel literally ceased to exist.[2]

Her people were dispersed among the nations. Her national homeland, desolate and in ruins, was under the control of others, just as God said. You can read about it in the history books.

The Miracle of Israel's Preservation

Now, it's a fact that when a people are deprived of a homeland and dispersed for any length of time, they soon lose their national identity. It happens even when the dispersal is voluntary. The melting pot that is America is a graphic illustration of this. People from England, Ireland, France, Germany, Holland, Poland, Mexico, Vietnam, Cambodia—the world—have come to America. And in 200 years there has been, and continues to be, such a blending of nationalities and races that a new people has emerged.

In many of the South American and Southeast Asian countries, this kind of blending has, in just 300-400 years, made it difficult to detect original ancestries.

But consider the Jews!

Deprived of self-government for some 2,500 years and without a national homeland for nearly twenty centuries, they have still maintained their distinctive nationality.

The magnitude of this phenomenon is increased when the Jews are compared to other contemporary nationalities. Where are the Assyrians, the Babylonians, the Hittites or Amalekites today? They were great nations at one time, often controlling the then-known world. In fact, at the time when the Jews were conquered by the Babylonians, it is estimated that they numbered less than a million, while their captors were many times that population. Yet today, even as the Jew lives on, many of these other nations are gone.

Mark Twain, certainly not a religious man, observed and commented on this amazing phenomenon. He wrote:

> He [the Jew] could be . . . vain of himself and not be ashamed of it. Yes, he could be excused for it. The Egyptian, the Babylonian, and the Persian arose, filled the planet with sound and splendor, then faded to dream-stuff, and passed away; the Greek and the Roman followed, and made a fast noise, and they are gone; other peoples have sprung up and held the torch high for a time; but it burned out, and they sit in twilight, or have vanished. The Jew saw them all, and is now what he always was, exhibiting no decadence, no deformities of age, no weakening of his parts, no slowing of his energies, no dulling of his alert, aggressive mind. All things are mortal but the Jew; all other forces pass, but he remains. What is the secret of his immortality?[3]

The secret is that God has spoken concerning the Jew, and He is keeping His Word supernaturally.

The Miracle of Israel's Nationhood

Besides retaining his national identity, miraculous as that is, the Jew has regained and is again, against unbelievable odds, in his original homeland.

After the Jews were dispersed, a succession of nations controlled Palestine. The Romans ruled until A.D. 611 when the Persians swept over the land. They in turn gave way to the Islamic armies of Saladin in 637, during whose rule the Muslim Dome of the Rock was constructed in Jerusalem.

The Crusaders captured Jerusalem in 1099 and held it till 1187, when the Muslims of the area recaptured it. The Ottoman Turks overpowered them in 1291 and held the land until December of 1917, when General Allenby and his British forces captured Jerusalem without firing a shot. World War I thus opened Palestine for the return of the Jews.

Meanwhile, in the late nineteenth century, the Jewish nationalist movement known as Zionism was born in Eastern Europe. The Jews, who had often suffered violence in various places through the centuries, lived in fear of the periodic Russian pogroms. When brutal massacres were finally unleashed, the drive for a return to Palestine accelerated.

It had to be Palestine. In 1903, the British government offered the Zionists territory in Uganda, then a British possession. They turned it down, emphatically insisting that they must return to the promised land of their forefathers—Palestine.

Some began to return. By the end of the 1800s there were approximately 5,000 Jews in Palestine, pioneers who settled in marshlands and barren areas purchased from absentee Arab owners. The earliest Jewish towns and villages were built by them from 1880 to 1922. Deganiah (The Cornflower) was founded by ten men and two women as the first kibbutz (Jewish collective settlement). It became the forerunner of nearly 400 such present-day collectives. Begun on a swampy fringe of the Jordan River, Deganiah, surrounded by orchards, gardens and green fields of corn and vegetables, today stands as a showpiece of modern Israel.

By 1914, the Jewish population had risen to 85,000. In 1916, when the area was the theater of furious fighting during World War I, the British were given control of Palestine and Iran under an agreement with France.

When General Allenby captured Jerusalem in 1917, the Balfour Declaration was put into effect. In this historic document, Britain said she would "view with favor the establishment in Palestine of a natural home for the Jewish people and would use her best efforts to facilitate the achievement of this objective."

However, when Jews began to return in slow but steadily increasing numbers, tensions between them and the Palestinian Arabs frequently erupted into overt conflict. In 1939, Britain, frustrated by the conflict, issued a White Paper that favored Arab independence and control. Of course, the horrors of the Holocaust during World War II convinced vast numbers of Jews that they must have a national homeland for the sake of security. The pressure grew. Nevertheless, in 1946, immigration of more Jews was forbidden and finally, in 1947, the British withdrew from Palestine.

Immediately hostilities flared between the Jews and Arabs. The United Nations stepped in, partitioned the country and sought to keep the peace. Shortly thereafter, the Jewish National Council and the General Zionist Council proclaimed from Tel Aviv the establishment of the sovereign State of Israel. David Ben Gurion was appointed prime minister and Dr. Chaim Weizmann was elected president of a provisional council.

Both the United States and Russia recognized the new nation which, after much debate, was accepted as a member of the United Nations. And so, on May 14, 1948, Israel became again a nation with her own homeland and national flag.[4]

The Miracle of Israel's Survival

But the miracle did not end with Israel's achievement of nationhood. The young nation's survival through five devastating wars is certainly as great a miracle, if not greater. Immediately after Israel's declaration of independence and statehood, the small, weak and newly formed nation of less than three-quarters of a million people was plunged into a life-and-death struggle for its very survival. The neighboring Arab states were not and, in most cases, have not since been willing to acknowledge Israel as a sovereign state with a right to Palestine. They attacked Israel militarily.

It should have been no contest. The massive documentary, *O Jerusalem* by Larry Collins and Dominique LaPierre, graphically tells the story.[5] In the natural, Israel didn't have a hope. The odds against her were overwhelming—and still are.[6]

But when the "war of independence" ended on January 7, 1949, Israel had not only survived, she had substantially increased her possession of key areas of the country. The U.N. came in to patrol a "no man's land" buffer zone between the Israelis and the Arabs.[7]

However, military and political pressures between the combatants steadily intensified until October 29, 1956, when Israel invaded the Sinai shortly after Egypt nationalized the Suez Canal and denied Israel's ships passage. The invasion, supported by Britain and France, was a complete success from the Jewish point of view. In just seven days, before the U.N. established the first international police force to supervise a truce, Israel routed 40,000 Egyptian troops, overran the Sinai and closed the Canal.

Once again a shaky peace ensued, but the build-up of tension soon began. The inevitable eruption came in June 1967 in the famous Six-Day War. That phenomenal Israeli blitz, against overwhelming odds in terms of manpower and military equipment, saw the Jewish occupation of the entire Sinai, the Golan Heights in Syria, the territory to the Jordan River and, most significantly, the Old City of Jerusalem.

Thus, in 1967, for the first time in over 1,900 years, the Holy City with its temple site, was in Jewish hands. Shortly after the capture of Old Jerusalem, and while the war was still on, General Moshe Dayan marched to the Wailing Wall, that last remnant of the old temple, and said, "We have returned to our holiest of holy places, never to leave again." The prophetic significance of this is enormous, as will be shown later in Chapter 12.[8]

Miraculous!

But perhaps the greatest evidence of the miraculous survival of Israel came in the 1973 Yom Kippur War. Many observers believe that war should have seen the annihilation of Israel. Even the then prime minister, the late Golda Meir, said of that conflict, "For the first time in our 25-year history, we thought we might have lost."[9] At one point, only a few battered Israeli tanks stood between the powerful Egyptian army and Tel Aviv. At the same time, the Syrian-amassed tanks had all of Galilee at their mercy, with virtually nothing to stop them from advance.

The Israelis had apparently become overconfident following their previous confrontations with the Arabs. The prevailing attitude was, "All you have to do is fire a few shots in the air and the Syrians run like rabbits. Just point a tank in the direction of Cairo and the Egyptians collapse immediately."[10]

So Israel was taken by surprise. The attack came on the Jewish high holy day. Many in the nation of Israel were observing the day in the synagogues or in prayer and fasting. With the Arab forces united for the first time in centuries, powerfully equipped with the latest sophisticated weapons and attacking on two fronts simultaneously, it appeared that Israel was indeed beaten.

The Arab assault was massive. In the north, the Syrians threw 1,200 tanks into a twenty-mile front, twenty-five percent more tanks than the Germans used in a 200-mile offensive against Russia in 1941![11] What has been called "the greatest tank battle in world history" was fought in the Sinai. According to news reports at the time, approximately 4,000 tanks, over 2,000 heavy guns, hundreds of missile batteries, 1,500 aircraft and nearly 1 million men as well as many new weapons were thrown at Israel at the start of the conflict. It was the Middle East's first truly technological war.[12]

Not only were the Israelis vastly outnumbered, but the Arab

weapons were superior, including the very latest Surface to Air Missiles (SAM) and other newly developed weaponry which had been supplied by Russia. In addition, massive Soviet airlifts of arms to Syria and Egypt began on the first day of the war. Two hours after the fighting started, Russian Antonov air transports, carrying weapons and replacements, began landing every three minutes at Syria's airport. Russian supply ships also came into port in both countries.

As for Israel, their help via the American airlift did not begin until the tenth day of the war due to the refusal of America's allies to grant facilities to the U.S. for the refueling of planes. When the U.S. planes finally did arrive, the Israeli army was literally running out of ammunition.[13] Israel's casualties in the first few days of the war were enormous. A comparable loss in the U.S. would have been 200,000 lives.

To fully tell the entire story of Israel's "miracle" survival and victory (of sorts), including the account of how the U.S. and Russia went to the very brink of nuclear war over the conflict, would take an entire book.

In fact, several have been written. Among them is one by Lance Lambert, a British citizen who was in Israel during the war and now lives there. He vividly, but in a sane and balanced way, describes that miracle in *Israel: A Secret Documentary*.

There is no logical explanation for the failure of Egypt and Syria to totally destroy Israel during the early days of the Yom Kippur War or for Jordan's refusal to attack—factors which undoubtedly would have been decisive.

The fact is that, after the Egyptians had taken the supposedly invincible Bar-Lev line in a third of the time they had projected for its capture, and after the Syrian tanks had a clear run into Israel from the Golan Heights, they both inexplicably just stopped.[14] Many feel that those unexplainable delays gave Israel the time it needed to recover, regroup and reorganize and likely made the difference in the outcome of the war.

Whether this is true or not, the fact remains that Israel's very survival through the Yom Kippur War was a miracle. Many Israelis agree: It had to be God.

Operation Peace

In June of 1982, Israel initiated war once again. The Israel Defense Forces (IDF) invaded Lebanon in an effort to destroy, once and for all, the Palestinian Liberation Organization (PLO) army. That international terrorist force, dedicated to the destruction of the state of Israel, had become deeply entrenched in Israel's neighboring nation, Lebanon. It had become a base from which PLO terrorist attacks on Galilee were regularly launched.

The effort was dubbed "Schlomal Galilee"— Operation Peace for Galilee.

Israel's military objective—the defeat and dislodgement of the PLO from Lebanon—was achieved. In late September of 1982, the remnant of the PLO army left Beirut to be dispersed to the various Arab nations which would allow them entry. However, in the aftermath of the war, Israel suffered a severe propaganda defeat, being made to appear "inhumane" by much of the world media because of her perceived role in the brutal October massacre of hundreds of refugees in a Palestinian camp.

Since then, much has happened. Following years of turmoil, terrorism and conflict between the Palestinians and Israelis, Iraq's Saddam Hussein attempted to unify the entire Arab world against Israel during the Gulf War of 1990-1991. Though no government of any Arab nation supported Hussein, his call met with a high degree of response from the rank and file of Arabs in many countries.

In 1994, the improbable occurred.

After months of posturing and behind-the-scenes negotiation, Israel and the PLO signed a peace accord which in effect saw Israel agree to trade land for peace.

The accord and its partial implementation have created enormous opposition among the Israelis who fear it is the beginning of a "slice by slice" strategy to destroy their nation.

Nevertheless, the fact remains that Israel is very much a modern-day nation. And, according to the International Institute for Strategic Studies (the definitive authority on armaments), the Israelis are the world's fourth most powerful military force, an incredible achievement for so small a nation. In spite of the continuing external pressures and the enormous burden of maintaining such a huge military, Israel has grown in strength and stability through its brief but turbulent modern history.

The Miracle of Her Productivity

A less dramatic, but nonetheless real, miracle is the fulfillment of prophecy concerning Israel's productivity after centuries of desolation. The prophetic word to Israel foretold desolation upon the land because of their disobedience.

> If in spite of this you still do not listen to me but continue to be hostile toward me . . . I will lay waste the land, so that your enemies who live there will be appalled.
>
> I will scatter you among the nations and will draw out my sword and pursue you. Your land will be laid waste, and your cities will lie in ruins. (Leviticus 26:27, 32-33)

> [T]herefore, O mountains of Israel, hear the word of the Sovereign LORD: This is what the Sovereign LORD says to the mountains and hills, to the ravines and valleys, to the desolate ruins and the deserted towns that have been plundered and ridiculed by the rest of the nations around you. (Ezekiel 36:4)

For hundreds of years Palestine truly was desolate. Mark Twain's verdict after his visit there in the 1870s was "forbidding desolation." Erosion, deteriorating terrains, malarial swamps, with little vegetation to be found anywhere—this was the description he gave. Very few habitants were in the land—exactly as prophesied.

However, restoration was also foretold.

> But you, O mountains of Israel, will produce branches and fruit for my people Israel, for they will soon come home.
>
> I am concerned for you and will look on you with favor; you will be plowed and sown. . . .
>
> I will increase the number of men and animals upon you, and they will be fruitful and become numerous. I will settle people on you as in the past and will make you prosper more than before. Then you will know that I am the LORD. (Ezekiel 36:8-9, 11)

> I will save you from all your uncleanness. I will call for the grain and make it plentiful and will not bring famine upon you.
>
> I will increase the fruit of the trees and the crops of the field, so that you will no longer suffer disgrace among the nations because of famine. . . .
>
> The desolate land will be cultivated instead of lying desolate in the sight of all who pass through it.
>
> They will say, "This land that was laid waste has become like the garden of Eden; the cities that were lying in ruins, desolate and destroyed, are now fortified and inhabited." (36:29-30, 34-35)

It's Happening in Our Time

The foreshadowings of fulfillment for these prophecies appear to be coming true in our time. Since Israel achieved statehood, millions of trees have been planted, covering hundreds of thousands of acres. Swamps have been drained, sand dunes anchored with vegetation, erosion combatted, soil improved and massive irrigation undertaken. Agriculture has been modernized and crops of corn, wheat, cotton, peanuts, sugar beets and nuts are harvested. The nation produces more than seventy percent of its own food supply.

Israel has also become the world's second largest producer of grapefruit, and her Jaffa oranges are world famous. Grapes, bananas, dates, lemons and other fruit are grown and exported, as well as enormous quantities of vegetables. The Isaiah 27:6 pronouncement, "Israel will bud and blossom and fill all the world with fruit," appears to be seeing fulfillment.

Other products include olives, almonds, figs, apricots and pomegranates. Flowers and flower bulbs are also grown and exported by the hundreds of millions each year.[15]

In addition, Israel, which now has a population approaching 4.5 million, over one-third of whom are native-born *sabras*, also has very progressive mineral and manufacturing industries and produces about ten percent of her oil needs. She is very active in solar energy research and development and maintains aggressive oil exploration, which has experienced good success.

What's the Point?

The point of all of this is that, in a very special way, a re-gathered, prosperous nation of Israel is the most significant sign of prophecy's impending fulfillment. Luke 21:29-32 is the record of the parable Jesus told about the fig tree (the historic symbol of national Israel) putting forth its leaves, indicating that summer was near. Jesus told that parable as part of His answer to the disciples' question, "[W]hen will this happen, and what will be the sign of your coming and of the end of the age?" (Matthew 24:3).

In the first part of His answer to those questions, Jesus described many general world conditions like wars, famines and earthquakes which He said would increase in frequency and intensity like labor pangs prior to the birth of a child.

Then, as a major part of His response, Jesus spoke of Israel. He foretold that, following a lengthy worldwide dispersal, the Jews would return to the land of Palestine, the temple would be rebuilt and their ancient worship would be restored (Matthew 24:15, 16, 20).

Finally, He foretold that the generation which saw Israel reborn "will certainly not pass away until *all* these things have happened" (24:34, emphasis mine).

So, the miracle of Israel's rebirth has occurred. In spite of all the odds against it, Israel exists and will continue to do so supernaturally. Read Jeremiah 31:35–36 for the guarantee from God!

Just as the appearance of leaves on the trees is a sure sign that summer is near, so the emergence of Israel and its position as the world's hot spot is a clear indication that Jesus Christ will soon return and that the culmination of earth's history will take place.

The budding of the fig tree—a Jewish nation reborn in Palestine and controlling for the first time in more than two millennia the city of the temple—is the key piece of the prophetic jigsaw puzzle slipping into place and making possible the placement of the many adjacent pieces.

It's an exciting time to be alive!

Notes

1 *Encyclopedia Britannica* (William Benton, Pub.), 1978 Edition, Vol. 13, p. 8; Vol. 17, pp. 130–136.

2 Micha Livnek and Ze'ev Meschel, "Masada," a publication of the National Parks Authority of Israel, Nov. 1965, pp. 16–17.

3 Mark Twain, as quoted from *The World's Greatest Library* in *The Beginning of the End*, T. LaHaye, ed. (Wheaton, IL: Tyndale House Publishers, 1972), p. 44.

4 C. Pack, ed., *Dry Bones: Two Sticks and Falling Dominoes* (Oklahoma City, OK: Southwest Radio Church, 1974), pp. 8–41.

The massive buildup of military might by Iraq and other Mideast

Arab nations prior to the Gulf War of 1991 and since continues to maintain a major imbalance.

5   L. Collins, D. LaPierre, *O Jerusalem!* (New York: Pocket Books, 1973), pp. 243–435.

6   A USAF intelligence report, published in the 1979 Report to the National Committee on American Foreign Policy, said that over the preceding fifteen years Arab manpower outweighed Israel's by ten to one, armor by at least five to one, assault weaponry and artillery by five to one or higher, combat aircraft by three to one, munitions stocks and military production ratios by 100 to one.

7   *The Beginning of the End*, pp. 45–54.

8   L. Latham, *Israel: A Secret Documentary* (Wheaton, IL: Tyndale House, 1975), p. 9.

9   Ibid., p. 58.

10 Ibid., p. 12.

11 Ibid., p. 13.

12 Ibid., p. 17.

13 Ibid., p. 15.

14 Pack, pp. 8-15.

15 Ibid., p. 16.

"On the mountains of Israel you [Gog] will fall, you and all your troops and the nations with you."

—Prophet Ezekiel, 2,600 years ago

CHAPTER 12

The Bear Pounces—into a Trap!

Russia is going to invade Israel. It is not a question of *if*, in spite of the collapse of the Soviet Union, but *when*.

However, the big Bear's pounce upon tiny Israel will result, not in the annihilation of the Jews, but rather in the defeat of Russia's war machine—a seemingly unlikely outcome which will create the power vacuum that precipitates the rise to world power of earth's final global dictator.

If this sounds like an incredible and completely implausible scenario, stick around for the documentation. It's all been foretold by those "100-percent-accurate" prophets. The pieces are now starting to fall into place.

Ezekiel Has a Vision

First of all, let's look at what the prophet Ezekiel wrote some 2,600 years ago. Chapter 37 of Ezekiel's prophecy contains the account of a valley of dry bones—skeletons of a defeated army. Ezekiel was told by God to preach to the bones. When he did, they began to come together with sinews and flesh appearing, then breath, then life. A mighty army.

Then he said to me: "Son of man, these bones are the whole house of Israel. They say, 'Our bones are dried up and our hope is gone; we are cut off.'

"Therefore prophesy and say to them: 'This is what the Sovereign Lord says: O my people, I am going to open your graves and bring you up from them; I will bring you back to the land of Israel.

" 'Then you, my people, will know that I am the LORD, when I open your graves and bring you up from them.

" 'I will put my Spirit in you and you will live, and I will settle you in your own land. Then you will know that I the LORD have spoken, and I have done it, declares the LORD.' "

The word of the LORD came to me:

"Son of man, take a stick of wood and write on it, 'Belonging to Judah and the Israelites associated with him.' Then take another stick of wood, and write on it, 'Ephraim's stick, belonging to Joseph and all the house of Israel associated with him.'

"Join them together into one stick so that they will become one in your hand.

". . . [A]nd say to them, 'This is what the Sovereign LORD says: I will take the Israelites out of the nations where they have gone. I will gather them from all around and bring them back into their own land.

"I will make them one nation in the land, on the mountains of Israel. There will be one king over all of them and they will never again be two nations or be divided into two kingdoms.

" . . . They will live in the land I gave to my servant Jacob, the land where your fathers lived. They and their children and their children's children will live there forever, and David my servant will be their prince forever." (Ezekiel 37:11-17; 21-22; 25)

In Chapter 11 I suggested that this prophecy was in the beginnings of its fulfillment as Israel has become once again a nation gathered out of over a hundred countries. There can be no doubt that Israel, which as we'll see in a moment is the target of a military attack, is the nation in view in this prophecy.

There's More

But Ezekiel was given a further prophetic insight, recorded in Ezekiel chapters 38 and 39. This is such a significant portion of Scripture that I urge you to get a Bible and read chapters 37, 38 and 39. For convenience, however, portions of it are reproduced here.

The word of the LORD came to me:
"Son of man, set your face against Gog, of the land of Magog, the chief prince of Meshech and Tubal; prophesy against him and say: 'This is what the Sovereign LORD says: I am against you, O Gog, chief prince of Meshech and Tubal.

" 'I will turn you around, put hooks in your jaws and bring you out with your whole army—your horses, your horsemen fully armed, and a great horde with large and small shields, all of them brandishing their swords.

" 'Persia, Cush and Put will be with them, all with shields and helmets,

" '[A]lso Gomer with all its troops, and Beth Togarmah from the far north with all its troops—the many nations with you.

" 'Get ready; be prepared, you and all the hordes gathered about you, and take command of them. . . .'

"Therefore, son of man, prophesy and say to Gog: 'This is what the Sovereign LORD says: In that day, when my people Israel are living in safety, will you not take notice of it?

" 'You will come from your place in the far north,

you and many nations with you, all of them riding on horses, a great horde, a mighty army.

" 'You will advance against my people Israel like a cloud that covers the land. In the days to come, O Gog, I will bring you against my land, so that the nations may know me when I show myself holy through you before their eyes.' " (38:1-7, 14-16)

For centuries, students of prophecy have believed that the great northern power which leads a confederacy of allies in an attack upon Israel is Russia. *The Destiny of the Nations*, written in 1864 by Dr. John Cumming, outlined this view long before Russia was a major power.

What are the reasons for believing that the northern power which leads the attack is Russia? There are at least three.

1. *The meaning of the names used.* Josephus, the most famed of ancient Jewish historians, held this view based on the fact that Genesis 10:2 lists Magog as the second grandson of Noah. History records that he and his descendants moved to and settled north of the Black Sea.

Tubal and Meshech, the fifth and sixth grandsons of Noah, moved south of the Black Sea. Intermarriage over the centuries followed. The descendants of Meshech and Tubal are identified as the Mushki and Tubali of the Volga River basin and present-day Moscow and Tobolsk.

The famous nineteenth-century lexicographer, Dr. William Gesenius, emphatically states that the word Gog could properly be translated "the prince of Rosh" and says that Rosh is definitely to be equated with Russia.[1]

Scofield's *Bible Notes*, the *Watson Bible Dictionary*, the *Schaft-Hertzog Commentary* and others support this view. Another extensive documentation for identifying Russia as Rosh is found in *After the Empire* by Mark Hitchcock.[2]

2. *The homeland location of the leader of the invaders.* Ezekiel 38:15 says that the invader will come "from [his] place out of

the north parts" (KJV), or, as it is rendered in some translations, "out of the uttermost north."

Now, remembering that compass directions in the Bible are always given in reference to the Holy Land, we can identify the invader. There is only one nation which fits the description of being to the uttermost north of Israel, and that is Russia. To check this out for yourself, get a globe. Run a line from Israel to the North Pole. You'll discover that it passes almost directly through Moscow. Russia, and only Russia, is to the uttermost north of Israel.

3. *The character of her leader.* God says to Russia, through Ezekiel (as recorded in chapter 38:3): "I am against you, O Gog." Such a statement seems contrary to God's very nature, for He is revealed in Scripture as being a God of love, mercy and patience. Could it be that God has set His face against Russia because of her anti-God stand and her persecution of the Jews?

For seven decades, she was officially anti-God. And, in spite of the recent changes, practical atheism is still the attitude of the vast majority of Russia's leaders and people.

Most serious of all was and is Russia's official treatment of the Jews. God has clearly indicated that Israel is His chosen people, and that "He who is not with me is against me." Though the Russian government has pursued somewhat more lenient relations with Israel, its history is one of anti-Semitism. Thus, Russia's cruelty to the Jews—second only to Hitler's—is believed to be a powerful reason for this indictment from God: "I am against you, O Gog."

The leader of the invasion, then, is Russia. But what about glasnost and the collapse of the Soviet Empire? We'll look at these questions later. First, let's complete a consideration of what is prophesied about the nations which join Russia in the invasion of Israel.

The Allies Line Up

Nearly 2,700 years ago God told Ezekiel to list the allies of the northern power which invades Israel. He did so in chapter 38:5–6, as follows:

> Persia, Cush and Put will be with them, all with shields and helmets, also Gomer with all its troops, and Beth Togarmah from the far north with all its troops— the many nations with you.

Who are these ancient nations on the political map at the end of the century?

Persia

There is no disagreement among scholars over what nation is the present-day Persia. This name, which figures prominently in ancient history, was changed as recently as March of 1935 to Iran. It should also be noted that the Persian empire included some, if not all, of present-day Iraq.

Cush

Ethiopia is a translation of the ancient Hebrew word Cush, according to Gesenius, and it is thus used in several Bible translations. Based on his scholarly conclusions, it is correct to say that the present-day Ethiopians make up a part of the Cushites.

Secular history also pinpoints Cush as the land south of Egypt, which is the modern-day Sudan. A reasonable view is that Ezekiel's Cush represents a number of present-day north African nations.

Such a conclusion coincides with the prophecy of Daniel 11 which speaks of the "king of the South," believed by some scholars to be a description of Cush or the African-Arab power bloc.

Put

Ancient Put is Libya. Gesenius' *Hebrew Lexicon* indicates

that the descendants of Put became the forefathers of the north African Arab nations such as Libya, Algeria, Morocco and Tunisia. This is supported by the clear declaration of ancient history such as Babylonian and Persian inscriptions and the statement of famed Jewish historian Josephus. The *Brown-Driver-Briggs Hebrew Lexicon* agrees.

Gomer

Gomer was the first grandson of Noah, as recorded in Genesis 10:2, and, according to tradition and history, migrated north up the Danube. He became the father of Ashkenaz, Riphath and the head of many families.

In the Jewish Talmud, Gomer is spoken of as Germani, that is, Germany. The present land of Germany was originally called "the land of Gomer" or Gomerland.

While it seems apparent that descendants of Gomer settled in what is known today as Eastern Europe, many of Gomer's people also settled at about 1200 B.C. in the southern Russian steppes along the north shore of the Black Sea. Later they were pushed out of southern Russia into part of modern Turkey and, though they went into decline as a national entity in about 600 B.C., it is commonly believed that they settled in what is today central and north-central Turkey.[3]

Togarmah

Many Bible scholars consider Togarmah to be Turkey, or the Turkoman tribes of northern Turkey and southern Russia. Gesenius identified Togarmah as a northern nation which was located in ancient Armenia, the northeast part of modern Turkey.[4]

The Political Position Today

Iran (Persia)

Author Mark Hitchcock writes,

Ever since the revolution and overthrow of the Shah in 1978, the nation of Iran has been one of the world's greatest troublemakers. The Iranians are Shiite Muslims, and contain the most radical branch of Islam in the world. The hatred of Iran for Israel is so obvious it requires no comment. As recently as June 1992, Iran was asked by Lebanon to rein in Hezbollah guerrillas in southern Lebanon. The Iranians responded by refusing and saying that Iran would use all of its power to back their war on the Jewish state.[5]

Following the Soviet breakup, Iran has sought to strengthen herself militarily by using her oil wealth to purchase weapons from Russia. An article in *The Jerusalem Post*, "The Russian-Iran Connection," says:

> What is known about Iran's conventional arming is . . . worrisome. Tehran is spending, according to Gates, at least $2 billion a year on arms. It is modernizing its navy, air force, and army. It has acquired Russian submarines, and it has sent submarine crews for training in a Russian naval base. In the hope of acquiring state-of-the-art weapons at bargain-basement prices, Iran has established close contacts with the Muslim republics of the former Soviet Union.[6]

The Muslim former Soviet republics referred to in the *Post* article are Kazakhstan, Uzbekistan, Kinghizian, Turkmenistan and Tajikistan. (All of these are in the area described by the prophet Ezekiel when he listed Russia's allies.)

Of particular significance is the fact that Iran has obtained three nuclear warheads—from Kazakhstan! Kazakhstan is one of three Muslim republics which have huge stores of intercontinental ballistic missiles and nuclear warheads. The fate of Russia's 30,000 nuclear warheads and 1.7 million weapons personnel is of critical importance. Hal Lindsey, in *The Final Battle*, writes:

The Russians, fearing an Iranian alliance with these southern neighbors, made a secret agreement with Tehran. I first heard about this from an Israeli general in the Mossad. It took the rest of the world eight months to find out about it, and most people still don't realize what happened. The agreement between Boris Yeltsin and Rafsanjani offered the best Soviet arms to Iran in exchange for a pledge not to evangelize these Muslim republics. Russia would help itself economically by making available to Iran some of the world's top technicians and scientists—including nuclear engineers—who were unemployed. Iran began with 273 of Russia's top nuke experts, many of whom are still working there.[7]

Meanwhile, the Central Intelligence Agency says that Iran will be able to produce its own nuclear weapons by the year 2000. In 1998 their acquisition of missile capacity able to easily strike Israeli targets caused an international furor. Obviously, Iran is not relying solely on the republics of the former Soviet Union for technical expertise in its quest for weapons of mass destruction. Another key strategic ally for the Islamic world in this regard is China.[8]

Ethiopia, Sudan (Cush)

According to Gesenius, Ethiopia is a translation of the ancient Hebrew word Cush. Based on his scholarly conclusions, it is reasonable to conclude that the present-day Ethiopians are part of Ezekiel's Cushites.

However, both secular and Hebrew scholars also locate Cush south of Egypt, in what is today the nation of Sudan. Ethiopia had a pro-communist coup in 1976 and has been firmly entrenched in the Russian orbit since. Her anti-Semite bias is clearly established.

Sudan is one of only a handful of Muslim nations governed by militant Islamic leaders. The de facto leader in the nation is chief of the National Islamic Front, whose declared goal is to make Sudan a militant fundamentalistic Islamic state. Sudan was one of the very few nations which supported Saddam Hussein in the Gulf War. Being violently anti-Israel, the present-day Cushites seem primed to join any attack on Israel.

Libya (Put)

Libya needs little introduction to the world today, having been a source of trouble and terrorism for both the West and Israel since Colonel Muammar Khadafy came to power in 1969. The protection from world justice of the two Libyan terrorists accused of the bombing of an international jetliner has been carried on in the face of sanctions.

Libya would jump at the chance to be part of an Israeli invasion. Khadafy's anti-Israel rhetoric makes this clear.

Turkey (Gomer)

Turkey has a reputation for being pro-West. But that may be changing. A *TIME* article by James Wilde quotes then-Prime Minister Suleiman Demirel as saying, "Turkey's position is more important than before. A new window of opportunity has opened for us with the Turkic republics. We are trying to include both the Balkans and the new Turkic republics."[9]

Recently, Turkey has experienced a rapid rise in fundamentalist Islamic power and consequently the government is clearly seeking to influence the former southern Soviet Islamic republics. The age-old linguistic, religious and emotional ties to these newly independent nations are being strengthened as Turkey seeks new prominence.

Surprising Absentee

As intriguing as is the list of Russia's confederates, an even more intriguing component in the mix is a nation that is missing from the list. The absentee nation is one which you would think, in the light of history, should be heading the group.

That unlisted nation is Egypt.

Ezekiel did not include Egypt in the lineup of nations he predicted would join Russia in her invasion of Israel, unless, of course, she is unnamed and included in the phrase "the many nations with you" (Ezekiel 38:6, 9). But historically, Egypt has been too important and too much of a traditional enemy of Israel to be relegated to the unnamed nation category in an umbrella phrase.

An historic event which occurred on March 26, 1979, may be the explanation for Egypt's omission from the list of invaders. On that date, Egypt and Israel signed a peace treaty.[10]

In New York City for a meeting that day, I picked up a newspaper whose front page was dominated by the headline "Let There Be No More Bloodshed," and by a huge full-color photo of the Egyptian President Anwar Sadat, Israeli Prime Minister Menachem Begin and U.S. President Jimmy Carter on the lawn of the White House, signing the historic document. The improbable agreement created a tremendous stir, much Arab and Russian opposition and many dire predictions that it could never be practically worked out.

However, it does seem to be working. The unprecedented April, 1982 withdrawal of Israel from the Sinai (won in war) and its return to Egypt was a major milestone on the road to full ratification of this truce between centuries-long and implacable enemies.

Of course, the treaty may fail yet to hold, and Egypt could still turn against Israel—thus becoming one of those unnamed "many nations with you" in the Russian-led invasion. Fundamentalist Islamics, both within and without Egypt, are putting great pressure on the government to become anti-Israel. The 1995 assassination attempt on the president is indicative of that pressure. So, the absentee nation could become one of the invaders.

However, Egypt's attitude and actions toward Israel during the 1991 Gulf War tend to support the view that the

Egyptian-Israeli peace treaty may hold and Egypt will not be among those end-time invaders.

But Can Russia Invade?

Many people, reacting to the breakup of the Soviet Union, have concluded that Russia is no longer an international threat. Her days as a true superpower are believed to be over. Her internal problems have mushroomed, with the Russian economy apparently in shambles, while throughout Eastern Europe the former Soviet satellite nations opted for democracy, though some have since elected communist governments.

So the general feeling has been that communism is dead. The West has won the Cold War and now needs to help its former enemies pick up the pieces. In fact, for a time it was believed that a "New World Order" was underway in which the U.S. and Russia would cooperate to police the globe and to insure an era of peace and progress.

Perhaps.

And perhaps not.

There are several reasons why conclusions such as the above need to be questioned and why the threat of a Russian-led invasion of Israel should not be written off. We'll examine these in Chapter 13.

Notes

1 D.W. Gesenius, as quoted in *The Beginning of the End*, pp. 63–64.
2 Mark Hitchcock, *After the Empire* (Oklahoma City, OK: Hearthstone Publishing, Ltd., 1992), pp. 44–45.
3 Ibid., pp. 46–47.
4 Hal Lindsey, *The Final Battle* (Palos Verdes, CA: Western Front, Ltd., 1995), p. 55.
5 Hitchcock, op. cit., p. 56.
6 *The Jerusalem Post*, May 30, 1992, p. 1.
7 Hal Lindsey, op cit., p. 55.

8   Ibid., p. 57.

9   James Wilde, "The Phoenix of Turkish Politics," *TIME*, February 10, 1992, p. 38.

10 *Today* (Gannet Westchester Newspaper), March 27, 1979, pp. 1, 14.

"Russia's interest in the Middle East precedes the advent of communism and is not about to disappear with [its demise]."

—The Jerusalem Post

CHAPTER 13

But Can He Still Pounce?

Russia's well-publicized woes, economically, politically and even militarily, have led many people to write off the former superpower as a candidate for the fulfillment of Ezekiel's prophecy.

To do so may not be wise.

There are at least four reasons why Russia should not be dismissed as the leader of an invading confederacy which comes against Israel as the Scriptures foretell.

1. *Change works both ways.* In light of the incredibly fast-moving and dramatic events of recent years in Russia and Eastern Europe, no one can say with certainty that equally rapid and dramatic changes in reverse could not occur. Ours is such a volatile world that virtually nothing can be ruled out! And Russia, as we have learned, is a country where anything can happen.

2. *Return to a dictatorship.* There is a well-documented fear

that a return to repressive rule in Russia, with the former communist goals intact, is possible. Soviet Foreign Minister Eduard Shevardnadze, who resigned in January 1991, did so in protest over his fear that a new Russian dictatorship was coming.

Prophetic writer Hal Lindsey comments:

> Many have thought that the fall of the Soviet Union totally eliminated Russia from the prophetic picture. However, the fall of the Soviet Union and the rise of the independent Muslim republics may actually give Russia a stronger alliance and stake in Islamic affairs.[1]

He then quotes the *Jerusalem Post*:

> What the West seems to have forgotten is that Russian interest in the Middle East precedes the advent of communism. It is not about to disappear with the demise of the Soviet empire. In fact, Russia has certain advantages in the regional power play. Communism's sweet promise may have lost its appeal for the region's oppressed peoples. But the rise of independent Islamic republics within the Russian orbit may become a far more effective weapon in the battle for their hearts and minds.[2]

Rampant crime, a crumbling economy and a seriously underpaid military have created the climate for a military coup against a physically weakened President Yeltsin.

An article entitled, "Is This Weimar Russia?" in the November 16, 1998 issue of *U.S. News & World Report* contained a startling set of comparisons between the German Weimar Republic of the 1920s—just before Hitler gained control—and the Russia of the late 1990s.

From hyperinflation and the response to it and the aftermath of a myriad of economic and social wars, the parallels are dramatic. The only difference is the apparent absence today—at least at the time of this writing—of a Hitler figure, although once popular politician Vladimir Zhirinovsky has aspired to be like Hitler.[3]

3. *A communist ploy.* Could the current glasnost be a ploy to gain help for their faltering economy which has been virtually destroyed by its burden of up to twenty-five percent military expenditure and the need to prop up the economies of her satellites?

In an article entitled, "Mesmerized by the Bear: The Great Soviet Deception, Part One," Donald McAlvany, editor of the *McAlvany Intelligence Advisor*, explores the rationale behind this concept of a fake glasnost. McAlvany maintains that the glasnost/perestroika ploy is not a new one. He lists five glasnosts prior to the current one: in the 1920s, 1936/37, 1941–45, 1956–59 and in the early 1970s.

The appearance of reform has invariably been welcomed by the West, with aid being provided in an effort to encourage any positive moves. Lenin in the '20s, Stalin in the '30s and '40s, Kruschev in the '50s and Brezhnev in the '70s—all received Western aid when it was believed that communism was moderating and that through the provision of aid the West could help in altering its harmful features, thus bringing in a new era of cooperation.

Unfortunately, each of the five previous thaws ended with a sudden crackdown by the Russians followed by renewed confrontation with the West.

Hal Lindsey, writing in *Countdown*, says of the current era:

> The reality is that the "collapse" of communism is part of a masterful game of deceit engineered by Mikhail Gorbachev and the Soviet KGB. It is part of an elaborate strategy to secure Western aid and technology, buy time, persuade the West to unilaterally disarm and, at the same time, continue a covert but nevertheless dramatic military buildup of its own.

What is taking place in Russia today was described . . .
before Gorbachev took power in a book written by a top
KGB defector. In *New Lies for Old* by Anatoliy Golitsyn,
the grand Kremlin deception was exposed.[4]

Golitsyn, who has been living in the United States under
an assumed name, was born in the Ukraine and raised in
Moscow. He studied at the High Diplomatic School, the
University of Marxism-Leninism and the KGB Institute. He
joined the KGB in 1945 and served as a staff officer, special-
izing in disinformation, until his defection to the West. He
was sentenced to death in absentia by the Soviet Judiciary.[5]

Golitsyn's seven major predictions of the Soviet long-range
policy, published in 1984, include these: the appointment of a
"liberal reformer" after Brezhnev and the staging of a spec-
tacular "liberalization" and move toward democracy; the "reform" of the KGB and granting of amnesty to dissidents;
release of East Germany to reunite with the West and the
dissolution of The Communist Warsaw Pact. Finally, the
move of former East Bloc (now "reformed") into membership
in the European Union.

This scenario, remember, was published in book form in
the U.S. in 1984, prior to the end of the Cold War and the
collapse of the Soviet Union in 1989-1990. And, with the exception of unsuccessful attempts at membership in the EU
by former East Bloc countries, the script has been carried out
to the letter.

4. *Rise of Islamic Fundamentalism.* Hal Lindsey in *The Final
Battle* writes:

Today, Communism appears to be on its way to the
ash heap of history. But a greater threat—a more evil
empire—is quietly, without fanfare, filling the void left
by the breakup of the Soviet Union. This movement
seeks not only to destroy the state of Israel but also to

overthrow the Judeo-Christian culture—the very foundation of our western civilization.

While Communism was only on the scene for seventy-five years, this evil empire is more than 1,300 years old. It once conquered most of the known world and its zealous adherents have never given up their imperial dreams. They have, like the Communists, at their philosophic core the sworn duty to "bury us."

The name of this movement—the greatest threat to freedom and world peace today—is Islamic fundamentalism.[6]

Lindsey quotes Joseph de Courcy, Jr., editor of the *Intelligence Digest* as saying: "Over the rest of this decade, the divide between radical Islam and the industrial democracies will become the most destabilizing factor in world affairs."[7]

Though ignored by most experts and much of the media, the rise of Islamic fundamentalism threatens most Muslim Middle East nations, sponsors uprisings or terrorism in many other nations and is spreading rapidly.

This new threat is actually billing itself as the successor to Marxism as the new agent of change in the world and the number one challenge to the Judeo-Christian world order.

Iranian President Akbar Hashemi Rafsanjani has publicly announced that the movement's goal is to unite all of the Islamic nations under the leadership of a coalition led by Iran and Syria. They see themselves as the pure expression of the real meaning of the Koran. Their first declared effort will focus on driving the West out of the Middle East, then to destroy Israel, liberate Palestine and reestablish Muslim authority over holy Jerusalem. The final goal is to replace the Judeo-Christian world order with a Muslim-based world order.[8]

It is intriguing to note that, though the Muslim world condemned Russia's 1994 invasion of predominantly Muslim Chechnya, the outcry was somewhat muted. Perhaps the rea-

Israel's potential invaders

son is that most of the Arab nations' military material is Russian-made, making continued technical material support and parts supply from Russia essential.

Many observers believe that the Muslims, being well aware of Russia's long-term designs on not only Middle East oil, but a warm-water port, such as the Persian Gulf would provide, are most willing to exploit these facts. It translates into an Islamic/Russian alliance which Islamic leaders perceive to be exactly what is needed to enable them to achieve their goals, particularly in regard to the destruction of Israel.

Yet another interesting fact is the 1998 appointment by Yeltsin of Yergeny Primakov as Russia's Prime Minister. Primakov, a former head of the KGB, is well-known as a hard-liner and, at one time, the Arab-speaking head of Russia's foreign intelligence network with strong ties to radical Islamic Middle Eastern governments. He is a longtime friend of Suddam Hussein and was a staunch supporter of Iraq during the Gulf War.

It is worth noting, as well, that five of the former Soviet republics are Muslim.

A Group of Protesters

Ezekiel foretells, in verse 13 of chapter 38, that there will be a feeble protest, uttered by Sheba, Dedan, the merchants of Tarshish and all her villages.

Who are they?

According to Dr. W.F. Albright in the *Bulletin of the American Schools of Oriental Research* published in 1941, Sheba and Dedan were land-bound traders located east of Palestine, while Tarshish was the leader of sea traders and marine merchants west of Palestine.

The term "Tarshish" came to be used as a synonym for any maritime power or area where mining, smelting and trading in metal ore was carried on. Great shipping interests got the nickname "Tarshish"; Ezekiel's Tarshish is evidently also a nation of merchants.

Because of this, Ezekiel's reference is believed to be an expression broad enough to take in all the younger nations of the Old and New Worlds, especially Britain and her former colonies.

This is reinforced by the fact that the protesters would have to be kindly disposed toward Israel, strong enough to at least protest and symbolized by a lion, or by a young lion (a colony). Perhaps Britain and her former colonies (including the U.S.) are in view here. Although this seems at best a rather tenuous identification and one which I offer simply as a possibility, it allows for the only scriptural reference to the U.S. or Britain.

It should be noted that these nations, whoever they are, apparently do no more than protest. No action is taken by them. Could such a response ever be true of the West—especially the U.S.?

After the Vietnam War, many observers felt that the U.S. will to resist aggression was gone. Its response to the Russian invasion of Afghanistan and other situations in the '80s appeared to support this view. However, reaction to the Iraq invasion of Kuwait and the ensuing Gulf War clearly demonstrated that isolationism was definitely not a U.S. stance in the early 1990s. The remarkably decisive, swift and massive military answer to the Iraqi aggression was spearheaded by the U.S. But not without a great deal of dissent.

It is my view that the aftermath of the Gulf War will be a swing toward isolationism by the U.S. Few conflicts will ever have as much reason to be called a "just war" as did the response to the Iraqi aggression, and if that war brought dissent and protest, a less justifiable one would likely be massively opposed. (This would be particularly true if U.S. casualties were to mount. The established tests for a "just war" are (1) being declared by a competent authority, (2) having a potential good that outweighs a potential harm, (3) being a measure of last resort, (4) having a justifiable cause such as the repelling of invaders and (5) having a reasonable likelihood of success.)

The public reaction to U.S. involvement is Bosnia is a case in point, as was the obvious town-hall opposition in early 1998 to a renewed attack on Iraq. Further, the decimation of the U.S. military under the Clinton administration and the diminished U.S. support for Israel further reinforces the view that there will be no intervention.

Reasons for Russia's Invasion

The question may well be asked, "Why would Russia invade Israel? Israel is really quite insignificant in size, with a population of only about 4.5 million. Why invade?"

The reason, according to Ezekiel, is that the invaders will think an evil thought of "taking spoil" (38:12, KJV). The words of the prophecy are:

> "This is what the Sovereign LORD says: On that day thoughts will come into your mind and you will devise an evil scheme.
>
> You will say, 'I will invade a land of unwalled villages; I will attack a peaceful and unsuspecting people—all of them living without walls and without gates and bars.
>
> I will plunder and loot and turn my hand against the resettled ruins and the people gathered from the nations, rich in livestock and goods, living at the center of the land.' " (Ezekiel 38:10–12)

The idea of a spoil (which means "booty or plunder taken or stripped in war") from Israel was, until recently, a foolish one. Palestine was a desolate, barren place called "the forbidding land."

But things have changed.

Since 1948, the desert has begun to "blossom like a rose." Lush fields replace barren landscapes. Agriculture has become a great industry, with Israel now the number one supplier of citrus fruits to Europe. Four crops a year of many vegetables are produced.

There is an abundance of copper in Israel. And the Dead Sea, with its incredibly rich mineral deposits valued by some sources as high as $13-15 trillion U.S., contains strategic deposits of potash (used for fertilizer), bromide (useful in oil production), magnesium (a possible replacement for aluminum) and lithium (a uranium replacement in nuclear processes)—to name but a few.

Israel also has oil capacity. Not only has there been optimistic and successful exploration, but one of the world's largest oil refineries is located at Haifa. Though the oil flow was turned off after 1973, the capacity is there, including two pipelines to the large seaports of Eilat and Ashdod. Those world-class ports are in themselves highly desirable factors from Russia's viewpoint. Israel's airport at Haifa, located at the head of the Valley of Megiddo, is one of the world's largest and most sophisticated. As such, it would be an important prize for Russia.[9]

More than this, Palestine is the "navel of the earth"—the land bridge between the three continents of Africa, Europe and Asia. Russia's alleged goal of world domination would be made much easier by the control of Israel, both through its location and its wealth. "Taking spoil" through an invasion of Israel could certainly be a very appealing prospect.

What about the Mideast Peace Treaty?

It is common knowledge, especially following Israeli Prime Minister Yitzak Rabin's 1995 assassination, that an Israeli-PLO peace process began in October of 1991. The accord, brokered by the U.S., was built upon a concept described as "land for peace" in which Israel would grant Palestinian rule over portions of the West Bank in exchange for assurances that the PLO and fellow travelers would desist from attacks upon Israel.

The process, which was shepherded through two Oslo Accords and which originally envisioned a completion of the agreement by December 1998, began to be implemented in its early stages in 1995. Israeli troops started withdrawal from villages and areas of the West Bank, turning the responsibility for control over to Palestinian police forces. However, the process was stalled for months over a variety of issues, acts of terrorism and other violence.

A new agreement was reached at a U.S.-brokered summit in October 1998. It was immediately denounced by groups in both the Israeli and the Palestinian camps.

The Arab terrorist organization Hamas publicly threatened Arafat with assassination, while the political right in Israel's Knesset vowed to bring down Netanyahu's government.

The entire effort has polarized the nation of Israel. Almost half the populace, some of them vehemently, oppose the idea, maintaining that it is simply the first step in a strategy by Yassar Arafat and the PLO to achieve their original goal of the complete destruction of Israel.

The extent to which the more radical Israeli groups hold such a view was tragically demonstrated when, in November 1995, Yigal Amir, right-wing Jewish student, assassinated Prime Minister Rabin. Amir has felt no remorse, convinced that he has done the nation a service, since he believed that Rabin, in leading Israel into the peace treaty, was a traitor.[10]

The reaction of many Israelis to the October 1998 agreement reinforced the fact of the severe Jewish polarization. At the time of this writing, the fall of Netanyahu's government was considered a possibility.

In the opinion of many, there is ample cause for concern over the wisdom of the kind of peace the treaty is designed to provide.

One faction in Israel believes that the peace process is doomed to failure because peace results only when a treaty removes the cause for conflict. This treaty does not do so, since the very existence of the nation of Israel in the Mideast is the cause of Arab and Islamic hatred. In the final analysis, concessions cannot suffice.

Sheik Tamimi, a leader of Islamic Jihad (holy war), wrote *The Obliteration of Israel: A Koranic Imperative* in 1990. In it he stated, "The Jews have to return to the countries from which they came. We shall not accede to a Jewish state on our land, even if it is only one village."

Yassar Arafat has frequently made statements which provide fuel for those who maintain the process is only the start of a PLO strategy to destroy Israel.

A typical example is a March 5, 1995, speech in Gaza in which Arafat said, "I tell you that a pledge is a pledge, to carry on the march until our children hoist the Palestinian flag over Jerusalem, the walls of Jerusalem, the minarets and churches of Jerusalem."[11]

Though removal from the PLO charter of the clause calling for the destruction of the state of Israel was a condition of the accord, this had not yet been done as of the end of 1998.

The historic ties which Russia has maintained over the years with Arafat and the PLO; the election of a Prime Minister such as Primakov, with his pro-Arab, anti-Israel stance and the pressure in Russia of nationally known politicians such as Zhirinovsky (author of a book about leading a Russian attack on Israel), all tend to support the view that an invasion of Israel by a Russian-led confederacy is a distinct possibility. (Please note the chart which presents a summary of the three end-time wars of which this invasion is the first.)

The Result

What will happen when Israel is invaded?

As has already been suggested, the invasion results in the crushing defeat of the northern confederacy, as Ezekiel's prophecy indicates:

EVENT	PARTICIPANTS	TIME	REASON	OUTCOME
First War Invasion of Israel Ezek. 38, 39	Russia and allies vs. Israel	Just before the Tribulation or possibly during the very first part of the first 31/2 years	Russia desires Israel's vast mineral wealth, oil and strate-gic location	God will intervene and through an earthquake in Israel plus supernatural rain and hail, five-sixths of the Russian army will be wiped out. It will take the Israelites 7 months to bury the dead and 7 years to collect and burn the debris.
Second War Armageddon Joel 3:9, 12 Zech. 14:1–4 2 Thess. 2:8 Rev. 16:13–16 Rev. 19:11–21	Armies from all nations vs. God and Israel	At the end of 7-year Tribula-tion period	Flushed with power, and furious over God's judgments in the Tribulation, the Antichrist will defy God, seek to destroy the nation of Israel and Jerusalem	The Lord Jesus Christ comes down from heaven and destroys, by His very appearance, the combined armies of more than 200 million men. The bloodbath covers 185–200 miles of Israel and blood is splashed "as high as the horses' bridles" (Rev. 14:20). Antichrist and the false prophet are cast alive into the fiery lake of burning sulfur (Rev. 19:20). Satan is bound in the Abyss for 1,000 years (Rev. 20:1–3).
Third War Final Rebellion Rev. 20:7–10	Satan and those deceived by him vs. God	At the end of 1,000-year Millennium period	God allows Satan one more oppor-tunity on Earth to preach his deceiving message in order to give those born in the Millennium a "Garden of Eden" choice	Satan will be successful in deceiving millions of those born during the millennial period to turn away from Christ. This horde of people will completely circle the believers and encompass Jerusalem in a state of seige. When this occurs God brings fire down from heaven, killing the multi-millions in Satan's army. Satan is then cast into the fiery lake of burning sulfur where the false prophet and Antichrist are, and they will be "tormented day and night for ever and ever."

Three end-time wars

I will turn you around and drag you along. I will bring you from the far north and send you against the mountains of Israel.

Then I will strike your bow from your left hand and make your arrows drop from your right hand.

On the mountains of Israel you will fall, you and all your troops and the nations with you. I will give you as food to all kinds of carrion birds and to the wild animals.

You will fall in the open field, for I have spoken, declares the Sovereign LORD.

I will send fire on Magog and on those who live in safety in the coastlands, and they will know that I am the LORD.

I will make known my holy name among my people Israel. I will no longer let my holy name be profaned, and the nations will know that I the LORD am the Holy One in Israel. (Ezekiel 39:2-7)

Apparently unusual natural disasters like earthquakes and upheaval, pestilence, torrential rain and hailstones combined with supernatural fire, brimstone and the outbreak of vicious fighting among the invaders themselves (38:21–22) will result in the destruction of five-sixths of the entire northern military force.

In addition, God says He will rain fire upon Magog (Russia itself) and on those who dwell in the coastlands. Some have speculated that this refers to nuclear destruction. It could be, but whether this is so or not, one fact is very clear: All the world will realize that the destruction of the Russian confederacy is the work of God, not man.

Exactly When Will It Happen?

Again, it is not possible to be dogmatic about the exact sequence of events. However, taking into account both Ezekiel's prophecy and that of Daniel in Chapter 11, the following scenario is one possibility:

Sometime after the Antichrist, head of the ten-nation confederacy, signs a seven-year treaty with Israel, the king of the South—the Arab bloc—will invade Israel (verse 40). At this point, the entire Russian confederacy will come down upon the Jews like a whirlwind, with chariots, horsemen and many ships.

Apparently the Russians will doublecross the Arabs, for Daniel 11:40–43 indicates that their hordes will enter not only Israel, but many countries including Egypt, Libya and Ethiopia which are specifically singled out. This fits the stated desire of the Russian leadership to control the entire Middle East because of its oil.

It is at this juncture that the nations (which could be the NATO powers) utter their feeble protest, to which Russia pays no attention whatever (Ezekiel 38:18).

At this point, the tidings from the north (of Africa) where the king of the North (the European Union) is at this moment in the prophetic preview, and from the east (the Oriental armies) cause the principal invader to set up headquarters in Israel.

Here, upon the mountains of Israel, Russia's war machine is destroyed.[12]

In Summary

One of the major political indicators of the climax of the ages is the prophesied alignment of the nations and the long-foretold invasion of Israel from the north. In spite of the apparent circumstances to the contrary in Russia, the Bible assures us that it is not a question of *if*, but *when*. Even now, the pieces are starting to fall into place.

Notes

1   Hal Lindsey, *The Final Battle* (Palos Verdes, CA: Western Front, Ltd., 1995) p. 36.

2   "The Russian-Iran Connection," *The Jerusalem Post*, May 21, 1992, p. 8.

3 "Is This Weimar Russia?", *U.S. News & World Report*, November 16, 1998, pp. 48-49.

4 Lindsey, op. cit., p. 132.

5 Ibid., p. 133.

6 Lindsey, op. cit., pp. 4-5.

7 Ibid., p. 6.

8 Ibid., pp. 221-224.

9 *League of Prayer Bulletin*, November 25, 1987, p. 3.

10 *The Patriot News*, Harrisburg, PA, February 22, 1996, p. A4.

11 *Countdown*, June 1980, p. 2.

12 Dave Breese, *The Mid-East Wars—Who Will Win?* (Hillsboro, KS: Christian Destiny, 1990), p. 21.

"[China] is a sleeping dragon. Let her sleep.
When she awakes, the nations will be sorry."

—Napoleon Bonaparte

CHAPTER 14

The Nations Are Stirring

Ours is a rapidly changing world, one in which relationships between nations, in particular, are very fluid. National alignments and friendships seem to lack the permanency of past eras when the world was less a global village than it is today, and the pace of international affairs was much slower.

Such conditions have prophetic meaning.

You'll remember, as noted earlier, that Jesus, in a message given on the Mount of Olives shortly before His crucifixion, likened Israel to "the fig tree" and other nations to "all the trees." He implied that just as the appearance of leaves on trees indicates the nearness of summer, so certain events in Israel and among the nations would signal the nearness of His return.

I believe that current volatile national alignments and developments are, at the very least, the beginnings of the "trees shooting forth their leaves," indicating that "summer is near."

We've already looked at the significance of Israel and at Russia's apparent preparations for an invasion of that nation.

Let's now consider some of the other nations and their activities to see whether or not they qualify as indicators of the impending climax.

The nations, or alignments of nations, which are described in the prophetic Scriptures in addition to Israel and Russia and confederates in her impending invasion of Israel, are these:

- the "revived" Roman Empire

- the "kings of the east" and

- the "princes of Ishmael" ("king of the South").

Let's examine these groupings of nations in the light of prophecy and current affairs.

The Empire Strikes Back

The prophecy of Daniel, including the foreshadowings of the fulfillment in the European Union, has been considered in Part One. In summary, that prophecy is given twice in Daniel, in Chapter 2 and in Chapter 7. The first was in a dream of a great statue and the second in a vision of strange beasts. These companion revelations depict empires, with the final empire (which is in existence at the time when the God of heaven establishes His never-ending reign) being identified as a ten-nation confederacy which emerges out of the fourth empire—the old Roman Empire.

As described earlier, the European Union began as a six-member economic partnership in 1957 in an agreement known as the Treaty of Rome. It has now become a fifteen-member power bloc which, as we have noted, has the potential to become the world's dominant entity.

The ultimate goal is a complete unification of Europe—in trade, economics and the political realm. Though it has experienced many internal problems, it is nevertheless steadily gaining in stability and power.

It is also interesting to superimpose a map of the Old Roman Empire over a map of the fifteen EU nations. There is a remarkable similarity! And while the current membership is undoubtedly not the final form of the revived Roman Empire, the EU must certainly be at least a forerunner of the final fulfillment of Daniel's vision—"trees putting out leaves" as "summer" approaches!

The Orient Factor

China, the world's largest nation with a population of some 1 billion, is considered by many to be another of the nations which is astir in accordance with biblical prophecy.

In the context of the three end-time wars predicted in the Bible (see chart on page 153), there are references to a massive eastern power. Revelation 16:12 refers to the "kings from the East" who come over the Euphrates to do battle in Israel at the time of Armageddon. In what many feel is a companion reference, Revelation 9:14-16 states that the number of the army is 200 million demonically energized people. Daniel 11:44 contains another reference to this eastern power which figures in end-time events.

To me, it is quite significant that Mao Tse-tung boasted on several occasions before his death that China could "field a people's army of 200 million militia." This is particularly interesting if it is remembered that, at the time when the apostle John penned his prophecy—some 1,900 years ago—such an army was absolutely unthinkable. Two hundred million was virtually earth's entire population at that time! For anyone to say that just one nation could have such an army was utter fantasy! Yet today it is a very real possibility.

China has nuclear capacity. In 1979, it completed the Karakoram Highway from Singkiang province down through Pakistan to the Indian Ocean. A spur of this highway goes through Afghanistan and Iran to Iraq, where the Euphrates River runs from Turkey to the Persian Gulf.[1]

It requires no great imagination to see that this great eastern power is no longer asleep, but appears ready, or gearing up, to play the role envisioned for her by the ancient prophets.

Those Intriguing Arabs

God has a plan for the Arab peoples as well. Abraham's son Ishmael, the forerunner of the Arab nations, received certain predictions and promises from God (Genesis 16:10-12 and 17:20).

God also said that Ishmael would be a wild man whose hand would be against every man, with every man's hand against him. God also said that he would become fruitful and multiply exceedingly; that he would beget twelve princes and would become great nationally, dwelling in the presence of his brethren.

These promises have seen at least a partial fulfillment. The Arab nations have been "wild"— that is, free and roving and fiercely independent. They have also been against every man in that they have traditionally been warlike and have spawned and experienced much military opposition throughout history.

Salem Kirban, a Christian Arab author and publisher, suggests in his *Reference Bible* that the twelve princes of Ishmael may well be the present-day peoples of Lebanon, Syria, Yemen, Jordan, Egypt, Saudi Arabia, Sudan, Libya, Algeria, Tunisia, Morocco and Iraq.[2]

The Arab bloc has become a factor in our era. Far from being the unimportant, backward desert countries which world opinion once held them to be, the Arabs are now a major consideration in global affairs. Oil has done it.

The twelve nations considered to be the "Princes of Ishmael" today control 3 million square miles of territory in which are to be found two-thirds of the world's proven oil reserves.[3] They comprise almost all of the OPEC nations, and whether they are raising the price of oil, as they did after the

1973 war with Israel, or forcing a glut and threatening to dump oil on the market, as they did in the early 1980s, or fighting among themselves, they are a significant factor in world affairs.

Terrorism

Terrorism is another area in which the Arab bloc has major global influence, admittedly negative. While not a policy of all Arab nations by any means, terrorism has nonetheless found a base within the Arab world, particularly Libya and Iraq.

A *U.S. News & World Report* editorial called Baghdad "the terror capital of the world."[4]

During the Gulf War, one of Saddam Hussein's threats was to unleash a global "war of terrorism" against the nations allied against him. He frequently appealed to Arabs and Arab sympathizers worldwide to engage in such activity. His close links with PLO's Yassar Arafat and other terrorists such as Abu Nidal gave substance to the rhetoric. The Pentagon reported the existence of over fifty identifiable terrorist groups at the beginning of the decade.[5] Numerous acts of terrorism in various places around the world did occur at that time and caused the leaders of nations to take the threats very seriously.

Libyan leader Colonel Muammar Khadafy has also been frequently quoted (as in the following Reuters dispatch) as saying, "If we have to export terrorism, we shall export terrorism." He has boasted of the capability to "export terrorism to the heart of America" and has often called on people in the U.S. to destroy that nation. Khadafy, like Hussein, has been consistently strident in his hatred for Israel. The U.S. State Department has often claimed that Libya is producing poison gas for a chemical warfare capacity.

The U.S./Libyan confrontations over terrorism erupted into a U.S. military strike at terrorist training bases inside

Libya in mid-1986. They were in reaction to a series of terrorist acts primarily (though not exclusively) against the U.S. and particularly against Jewish U.S. citizens.

But though the U.S. action against Libya had some effect, the specter of terrorism will not go away. In fact, as an Associated Press release from Washington, D.C., notes, "[T]he U.S. State Department has been quietly, but seriously, grappling with a horrifying long-range threat: the possibility that 'insane' terrorists may someday get their hands on an atomic bomb."[6]

The fear is real. The cover article of the January 1996 issue of *Popular Mechanics* was titled, "When Terrorists Go Nuclear." It described the fear that a terrorist group could obtain a nuclear device.

The same fear was thoughtfully addressed in a speech by Senator Richard Lugar, a candidate for the 1996 Republican nomination for President. Lugar outlined the very real danger of nuclear terrorism capable of destroying an entire city with a bomb in a suitcase. Some 400 instances of attempted nuclear smuggling of Russian materials were reported in the August 17, 1995 *Washington Post* review of Lugar's speech.

The Arab nations are, without doubt, part of the end-time stir among the nations.

But the fear is not just about nuclear devices. Even more unsettling is the specter of bacteriological warfare in which a terrorist with a tiny vial of lethal bacteria could slip into any major city and unleash deadly, devastating destruction on a massive scale. Iraq and Iran are said to be producing such biological weapons, as are Libya and Sudan.

Meanwhile, more conventional terrorism continues. In August of 1998, U.S. embassies in Kenya and Tanzania were bombed on the same day. Hundreds perished in the blasts. The attacks provoked a U.S. military strike by high-tech Tomahawk missiles against an alleged poison gas plant in Khartoum, Sudan and terrorist bases in Afghanistan.

The Afghanistan bases were reportedly the headquarters of the shadowy Osama bin Laden, a wealthy Islamic terrorist who is said to be the driving force behind Al Qauda, the umbrella organization of some twenty Islamic extremist groups led by him. bin Laden has been implicated in numerous terroristic attacks, including the World Trade Center bombing.[7]

In Summary

The "fig tree"—Israel, and "the other trees"—all of the nations or groups of nations mentioned in end-time prophecy, certainly are on the scene and in the news today.

It is not unreasonable to conclude that their existence and activities may be called the "putting forth of leaves."

Such a conclusion must mean that "summer"—the climax of earth's ages—is near, according to the political signs.

Notes

1   *The End Times Digest*, March 1980, p. 7.
2   S. Kirban, *The Salem Kirban Reference Bible* (Huntingdon Valley, PA: Salem Kirban, Inc., 1979), pp. 213-215.
3   *U.S. News & World Report*, February 18, 1991, p. 15.
4   *U.S. News & World Report*, March 12, 1992, pp. 32-35.
5   *The World Almanac and Book of Facts* (New York: Pharos Books, 1991), p. 516.
6   *Associated Press*, Washington, DC, June 25, 1995.
7   *U.S. News & World Report*, October 19, 1998, pp. 34-37.

The Climax of the Ages

Spiritual Signs

Satan always boldly attempts to counterfeit whatever God does. This drive will become surpassingly blatant at the time of the end.

Are there evidences in our day that the predicted end-time counterfeit spiritual entities are developing or are already in place?

Let's look in Part Three at spiritual signs of the impending climax of human affairs.

A satanic culmination of the spiritually adulterous religious activity of rebellious mankind is the final form of the counterfeit [church] system.

CHAPTER 15

Meanwhile, on the Religious Scene

Earlier, I introduced you to my Uncle Fred who occasionally visited my childhood home for several days at a time and loved to expound his prophetical views.

One topic in particular often recurred and tended to cause me a great deal of concern. My uncle had accepted, and thereafter strongly propounded, an interpretation of Revelation chapters 17 and 18 which has been held by some biblical students for many years. That view is that the "prostitute" of Revelation is a particular church (which shall be left nameless). Uncle Fred would wax eloquent "proving" how this was so and describing the dangers of it all. Consequently, I kept my distance from all members and aspects of that church because, even though I wasn't absolutely certain Uncle Fred was right, I wanted to be sure I was safe! I have since come to believe that the school of interpretation to which he subscribed was only partially right.

It Is a Church

The "prostitute" of Revelation is indeed a church. In fact, it is a powerful global religious system which will contain elements of Uncle Fred's designated church and many, many others. It will not be just one particular church or denomination.

Now, if all of this talk of a church being a "prostitute" and of a powerful global religion is confusing, I will explain.

Let's Define the Terms

A prostitute is a usually a woman who has debased her God-given sexuality in order to sell her body to any number of lovers. This is in direct contrast to a wife who becomes one with her husband in a faithful, pure union.

The man/woman relationship is frequently found in Scripture as a symbol of spiritual relationships. For example, the symbol used in Scripture to describe the Church (the body of born-again believers from around the world through the ages since Christ) is that of a bride.

In Ephesians 5 and Revelation 19, the Lord Jesus Christ is depicted as the Bridegroom, the One to whom the true Church will be married. We who are believers are the Bride of Christ whose union has not yet been fully consummated. In the Old Testament, Israel was said by God to have been married to Him (Isaiah 54:5–6) as a wife, with sin and straying being described as "adultery."

Spiritual departure from God is frequently symbolized in Scripture by the use of terms like "adultery," "whoredom," "harlotry." A woman is thus used symbolically in Scripture to signify religion.

A "good "woman, such as a bride or wife, means good religion, the true Church.

A "bad" woman, such as a prostitute, means an evil religious system that deceives the souls of mankind.

So when the prophet John used the term "prostitute" in

describing the vision he had received, he was writing about a religious system which had submitted its very existence to all that is contradictory to the true purpose God has established for the Church.

A Most Unusual Vision

Look at what John was inspired by God to write in Revelation 17. As you do, remember that the prostitute represents a false church, and the strange beast upon which she rides represents a confederacy of nations. Read the prophecy carefully and then consider its explanation.

> One of the seven angels who had the seven bowls came and said to me, "Come, I will show you the punishment of the great prostitute, who sits on many waters.
>
> With her the kings of the earth committed adultery and the inhabitants of the earth were intoxicated with the wine of her adulteries."
>
> Then the angel carried me away in the Spirit into a desert. There I saw a woman sitting on a scarlet beast that was covered with blasphemous names and had seven heads and ten horns.
>
> The woman was dressed in purple and scarlet, and was glittering with gold, precious stones and pearls. She held a golden cup in her hand, filled with abominable things and the filth of her adulteries.
>
> This title was written on her forehead:
>
> MYSTERY
> BABYLON THE GREAT
> THE MOTHER OF PROSTITUTES
> AND OF THE ABOMINATIONS OF THE EARTH.
>
> I saw that the woman was drunk with the blood of the saints, the blood of those who bore testimony to Jesus.
>
> When I saw her, I was greatly astonished.

Then the angel said to me: "Why are you astonished? I will explain to you the mystery of the woman and of the beast she rides, which has the seven heads and ten horns.

"The beast, which you saw, once was, now is not, and will come up out of the Abyss and go to his destruction. The inhabitants of the earth whose names have not been written in the book of life from the creation of the world will be astonished when they see the beast, because he once was, now is not, and yet will come.

"This calls for a mind with wisdom. The seven heads are seven hills on which the woman sits.

"They are also seven kings. Five have fallen, one is, the other has not yet come; but when he does come, he must remain for a little while.

"The beast who once was, and now is not, is an eighth king. He belongs to the seven and is going to his destruction.

"The ten horns you saw are ten kings who have not yet received a kingdom, but who for one hour will receive authority as kings along with the beast.

"They have one purpose and will give their power and authority to the beast.

"They will make war against the Lamb, but the Lamb will overcome them because he is Lord of lords and King of kings—and with him will be his called, chosen and faithful followers."

Then the angel said to me, "The waters you saw, where the prostitute sits, are peoples, multitudes, nations and languages.

"The beast and the ten horns you saw will hate the prostitute. They will bring her to ruin and leave her naked; they will eat her flesh and burn her with fire.

"For God has put it into their hearts to accomplish

his purpose by agreeing to give the beast their power to rule, until God's words are fulfilled.

"The woman you saw is the great city that rules over the kings of the earth." (Revelation 17:1-18)

What Does It Mean?

The two main figures in this prophecy are as fascinating as they are repulsive.

The prostitute is described as lavishly decked in jewels and gorgeous garments, holding a rich gold cup which is attractive on the outside, but full of putrefaction inside. Written across her forehead is the name "Mystery, Babylon the Great, Mother of Prostitutes and of the Abominations of the Earth." Most disgusting of all is the fact that she is drunk, but not with wine. She is drunk with the blood of saints and martyrs.

This brazen woman sits upon a seven-headed beast standing near a great body of water, with the seventh head having ten horns. The beast turns upon the prostitute, strips her and eats her flesh, finally burning her remains with fire.

Now, as I have suggested, this prostitute is the substitute for the Bride of Christ, the true Church. She will spiritually seduce not only kings (that is, she will not only wield control over the leaders of nations) but also mankind in general. This is clearly indicated by the explanation that the waters by which the prostitute sits "are peoples, multitudes, nations and languages" as the prophet specifically states in Revelation 17:15. All mankind, apart from the saints, is included.

Such a Perverse System

But what kind of religion could possibly hold such sway and gain such control over Muslims, Hindus, Christians (the nominal kind only, since I believe that the Church will have been raptured by this time), Buddhists, pagans, atheists and so on?

Quite apparently, no one religion like Christianity or Islam or Confucianism could get all the other religions to join it, though such attempts have been and are being made. Unquestionably, whatever religion it is, it will have to have a strong appeal, far stronger than the pull of watered-down liberal Christianity today.

What sort of religion could this be?

The solution to the mystery is found in the name on the prostitute's forehead: "Babylon the Great." The prostitute religious system is associated with Babylon, a city which was more than just a city. It was an entity which, as far as the world of its day was concerned, embodied in itself a world religion, a world empire and a world ruler whom all nations were compelled to worship as supreme. Thus, depraved religion, enforced by government decree and a sinful, lustful lifestyle, come to mind when Babylon is mentioned.

Proper biblical interpretation, which demands that the first meaning of a term in Scripture be followed in every successive use, confirms that we are close to solving the mystery of what religion the prostitute represents.

Babylon was born when the first world ruler, Nimrod (whose name meant "we will revolt") built Babylon on the Plains of Shinar in the process of constructing his kingdom (Genesis 10:8–10). The first united religious act undertaken by mankind was the construction of a tower whose top would "[reach] to the heavens" (Genesis 11:4). This was the famed Tower of Babel.

There has been much misunderstanding about this tower. Those first Babylonians were not attempting to build a tower which could actually reach the heavens. They weren't that stupid. Rather, they were building an astrological tower, a ziggurat, which could be used to study the stars, chart their courses, cast horoscopes and make predictions. *Halley's Bible Handbook* declares that idolatrous worship was the whole purpose for the construction of the ziggurats.[1]

The prophet Isaiah, in chapter 47:12–13, indicated that Babylon labored with magic spells and many sorceries since her childhood, that is, from the very beginnings of her history. Isaiah also prophesied that Babylon could not be delivered by her prognosticators, indicating that these practices were deeply ingrained in Babylon's life.

It is a fact that astrology, sorcery, clairvoyance, conjuring and magic had their origins in the writings of the Chaldeans who divided the heavens into the twelve sections of the zodiac and claimed that the stars control the destiny of mankind.

This religion reached its pinnacle in the Babylonian Empire. History reveals that each of the Babylonian rulers built giant ziggurats for the use of their astrologers and Chaldeans. They are still in existence today in Iraq. During the Gulf War, Iraqi airplanes were parked beside them in the belief that such historical sites would be spared and the planes would escape unscathed.

Daniel Adds Some Details

The book of Daniel lists the magicians, astrologers (conjurers), sorcerers and Chaldeans whom Nebuchadnezzar summoned to reveal his dream and its interpretation. These religious practitioners dealt in black magic, contact with demon spirits, materialization, witchcraft and astrology. According to Hal Lindsey in *There's a New World Coming*, the Chaldeans were a special priestly caste who could trace their family history back to the originators of the art of astrology.

The name Babylon, then, is synonymous with a false religious system which began there and which includes occultic practices.

The prostitute represents this religion. Her dazzling external appearance suggests the appeal the system has to the sensual nature. The gold cup full of putridness symbolizes the corruption of her teachings, while her intoxication with the blood of believers indicates her method of dealing with those who oppose her.

And, for the first part of John's prophecy, the prostitute rides or controls the beast. In other words, the religious system rules the nations. John is saying that an occultic amalgamation of the world's religions—the revived Babylonian religion—will control the final world power.

A look at Revelation 17:9 and 10 confirms this. Here's what the prophet says:

> This calls for a mind with wisdom. The seven heads are seven hills on which the woman sits.
>
> They are also seven kings. Five have fallen, one is, the other has not yet come; but when he does come, he must remain for a little while.

This tells us that the seven heads of the beast represent two things: seven mountains and seven kingdoms. The seven mountains undoubtedly refer to Rome—a city known around the world to be built upon seven hills.

The city of Rome in John's time was controlled by the Babylonian religious system. It was the center of pagan worship and was even called "Babylon" in Scripture.

They Are Empires

But the seven heads are also seven kingdoms or empires, and there's more information given about these. Note Revelation 17:10 and 12:

> They are also seven kings. Five have fallen, one is, the other has not yet come; but when he does come, he must remain for a little while. . . .
>
> The ten horns you saw are ten kings who have not yet received a kingdom, but who for one hour will receive authority as kings along with the beast.

Five of the seven kingdoms had fallen, one was in existence

at the time John wrote and one, the seventh, was yet to come. The seventh will be different from the rest, having ten horns.

The Seven Kingdoms

What does history reveal? Have there been seven kingdoms controlled by the religion of Babylon? No. So far there have been only six.

The Five That Are Fallen

The first of these was Assyria, with its capital of Nineveh given over to the occult as Nahum 3:4 reveals.

Next was Egypt, which has left us evidence of her preoccupation with the occult in those fabulously costly pyramids, all built according to astrological specifications. The sphinx is supposedly the key to the twelve sections of the zodiac.

Then there was Babylon, in which Daniel lived and served God. The Babylonian religious system reached its zenith, so far as the past is concerned, during the reign of this empire.

Medo-Persia conquered Babylon, but was in turn "enslaved by the Babylonian religion," as one writer has said.

The fifth of the five which had fallen by John's time was Greece, in which, as history reveals, occultic religion also held sway.

These empires all shared a common, underlying belief in astrology which bound together witchcraft, sorcery and magic. The practitioners of these arts usually enjoyed great stature and power, with kings seldom making any move without first consulting advisors steeped in Babylon's ancient occultic art.[2]

The One "That Is"

John referred to a kingdom that "is" (i.e., was in existence at the time of John's writing), which also came under the sway of the occultic beliefs which have their origin on the plains of Shinar at the tower of Babel. There can be no doubt that this was the mighty empire of Rome, whose dependence upon her augurs, sorcerers and astrologers has been immortalized in Shakespeare's Roman plays such as *Julius Caesar*.

The One That Is "Yet to Come"

This leaves only the seventh kingdom, the one described as "the other [who] has not yet come; but when he does come, he must remain for a little while."

Do you recall our discussion of Daniel's prophecy about the ten-nation confederacy arising out of the old Roman Empire? If we compare it with the ten horns of John's symbolic beast, it seems obvious that this kingdom, which will be influenced by the ancient religion of Babylon, is the revived Roman Empire— the European Union.

It is apparent that some in the EU make the Babylonian connection, as indicated by this 1989 official EU poster. It combines a representation of the tower of Babel with occultic pentagrams (upside down stars) as symbols of the EU member nations. The combination seems to be too obvious to be a mere coincidence. It is a reflection as well of the extent to which spiritualism of the occultic or New Age has impacted Europe.

Now, having provided this panorama of world powers seduced by the harlot, the prophet narrows his focus to the final world power—"the beast who once was, and now is not"—and says that this king will be destroyed (17:11).

John says he "is an eighth king." His destruction fits the picture we have sketched elsewhere when we recall that the Antichrist, who takes charge of the revived Roman Empire, later sets himself up as God.

This satanic culmination of the spiritually adulterous religious activity of a rebellious mankind is in effect the eighth and final form of this counterfeit system. But in deifying himself, the Antichrist will destroy the prostitute. Though the revived Roman Empire is initially controlled by the religious system (and the Antichrist apparently goes along with it), the two are strange bedfellows. Each is trying to use the other.

Thus, at the midpoint of the seven-year treaty, the Antichrist decides he no longer needs the false church. He and the False Prophet, energized by Satan, have become wonder workers in their own right. So, he proclaims himself to be God, and the prostitute is destroyed by him. How ironic!

Is there anything on the worldwide religious scene today that would cause us to believe that these events could occur in the not-too-distant future? I believe there is.

There are at least three trends which appear to be foreshadowings of the harlot's appearance. An examination of these is the subject of Chapter 16.

Notes

1   H. Halley, ed., *Halley's Bible Handbook* (Chicago: H.H. Halley, 1951), pp. 82–83.

2   H. Lindsey, *There's a New World Coming* (Santa Ana, CA: Vision House Publishers, 1973), p. 236.

"My greatest personal dream is to get a tremendous alliance between all the major religions and the United Nations."

—Robert Muller,
former Assistant General Secretary
of the United Nations

CHAPTER 16

Could It Be Soon?

Mystery Babylon—a strange mixture of the religious and the political. What events on the worldwide religious/political scene would lead us to believe that the prophecies of the Apocalypse about such an entity are nearing fulfillment?

There are at least three.

A One-World Church

First, there is a continuing drive for a one-world church united regardless of doctrine or even religion. At this point a brief dip into the history of an organization called the World Council of Churches is essential.

The World Council of Churches traces its roots to the Universal Christian Council on Life and Work held in Stockholm, Sweden, in 1925. Joint conferences between this Council and the older International Missionary Council resulted in the formation, in Amsterdam, of the World Council of Churches (WCC) in 1948.

The WCC meets every seven years in a General Assembly of delegates appointed by member churches or religious organizations. An 150-member Central Committee meets every six months, but the real power resides in the Secretariat in Geneva.

Dr. J. DeForest Murch says in *The Coming World Church* that the World Council of Churches "is composed of a wide assortment of churches which have great differences in theological doctrine, church organization and worship. They represent many nationalities, political viewpoints and sociological backgrounds. They are unitarians and trinitarians. . . . There are dozens of different rites and liturgies of communion and worship."

The aim of the WCC is an all-encompassing, global religious entity, as the following makes clear.

The Signs of the Times, under the headline, "Churches Building Bridges," said that "the movement to bridge gaps among the churches, to unite them all into one great super church, may not hit the headlines these days, but it is advancing with increasing momentum."[1]

The visit of Pope John Paul II to the Orthodox Ecumenical Patriarch Dimitrios in Istanbul; the Lima "convergence document," agreed upon by representatives of the Roman Catholic, Eastern Orthodox, Oriental Orthodox, Lutheran, Reformed, Anglican, United, Baptist, Methodist, Disciples and Adventist traditions; the moves toward Protestant union in the U.S.; the visit of the Pope to Canterbury Cathedral and a joint worship service there—all are indications of an accelerating push for church union within the Christian realm.

But Not Just "Christian" Union

Malachi Martin, in his monumental volume *The Keys of This Blood*, writes:

. . . the WCC decided in 1970 that the word [church] should no longer be confined to "church of the Christian faith," or even to believers. Rather it should encompass people of any faith, and of no faith at all. . . . Accordingly, it became a matter of principle for the WCC . . . to enlarge their "interfaith" meetings and "ecumenical" activities to include such ideas as would promote their adopted [aims].[2]

Consequently, consultations between the WCC and various other religions are now held. A case in point is the year 1982 in which two such meetings were held. The first was in Sri Lanka, March 30–April 1, and was jointly sponsored by the WCC and the World Muslim Congress of Karachi, Pakistan. It brought together representatives from thirty different Christian churches to confer with thirty-three Muslims. The consultation ended with a call for "the establishment of a joint Standing Committee between the World Muslim Congress and the World Council of Churches." A report of the meeting concluded with this statement:

> It is very much hoped that the joint Standing Committee could seek representation soon from other international Islamic organizations and from the Roman Catholic Church. This meeting certainly represented a historic first in the reconciliation process between Muslims and Christians.[3]

A second meeting that year was called by the WCC Unit on Dialogue with People of Living Faiths and Ideologies. It met in Hawaii to "grapple with the complex question of traditional cultures," including how to affirm these faiths and cultures.

"Theologians Take Steps in Dialogue with Men of Other Faiths" was the heading of a story by the Ecumenical Press Service, organ of the WCC . The story said:

"Christians must place their faith in Christ in a positive relationship to the faiths of other men if conversations between each other should neither betray the commitment of the Christian nor exploit the confidence of men of other faiths," 23 Christian theologians said here recently. They were attending a consultation on "Christians in dialogue with men of other faiths" which was a follow-up to the recent World Council-sponsored conference between Hindus, Buddhists, Christians and Muslims in Ajaltoun, Lebanon.[4]

If the concept of bringing together faiths with such widely divergent views as the ones mentioned in the foregoing news stories seems strange, the words of the WCC's First General Secretary, Willem Vieer't Hooft must be recalled. He said, "In the World Council, there is a new creation—churches agreeing to disagree on aspects of faith but committed to seeking its fullness together."[5] Accordingly, the World Council of Churches is the main organization working for dialogue with other religious and pagan faiths.

While the goal of a single global church has undoubtedly been in the minds of churchmen for many years, these concrete efforts to achieve it are of comparatively recent vintage. Now the amazing spread of the philosophy of secular humanism, defined in the Humanist Manifestos I and II, published in 1933 and 1973, has given this drive a powerful global push, especially in the West.

Martin, in *The Keys of This Blood*, presents a penetrating analysis of the various contenders for control of a one-world government. One grouping of globalists which he singles out includes "the Humanists, *the Mega-Religionists* [emphasis mine] and the New Agers." He identifies these as global activists and gives a masterful overview of their history and agendas, particularly that of the Mega-Religionists. He documents the involvement of the "Marxist WCC" and the inclusiveness of the movement. Their drive, as he sees it, includes

all major religions: Buddhism, Hinduism, Islam, Ju
Confucianism and Christianity.[6]

While Martin may not view these three elements as t
aspects of one entity, I believe they are all part of the prepa
tion for the full-blown manifestation of "Mystery Babylon.

I may offend some of my readers, but I am certain that th
global drive for a one-world church by what Martin calls "the
Mega-Religionists" is a forerunner, at least, of a major part of
the counterfeit church.

The UN Is Pushing It

This push for a global one-world religion (which in the
view of its current architects would be imposed on mankind)
has picked up speed in recent years. And it has done so in
conjunction with the religious aspects of the UN. Ominously
enough, the goal envisioned—a one-world government supporting and supported by a one-world religion and educational system, enforced by a global police/military—fulfills
two of the three elements of Mystery Babylon. Babylon embodied a world empire, a world religion and a world ruler
whom all were compelled to worship. Only a one-world ruler
would yet be needed to complete the picture.

The exceptionally well-documented book *Freedom on the
Altar*, by William N. Griggs, clearly indicates how this is
happening. Readers are encouraged to obtain and study this
excellent volume.

Grigg summarizes well the materials which I have collected over many months. They document the dangers of the
stated UN goals of global education through UNESCO, the
enforced population control and complete restructuring of
the family through UNICEF—highlighted most recently by
the UN Conference on the Family in China in 1995—and the
1998 effort to create an International Criminal Court. A
global religion is being developed.

Permit a brief overview.

rt Muller, a former UN Assistant Secretary General,
ggested that the "UN itself symbolizes the body of
t and that people worldwide should display the UN flag
ll houses of worship." He has said, "My great personal
eam is to get a tremendous alliance between all the major
eligions and the UN."[7]

Already the UN "Temple of Understanding," a foreshadowing of this proposed global alliance, stands on fifty acres by the Potomac River in Washington, DC. The architectural symbolism of the building is explained thus in a Temple brochure: "Radiating from [the] central hall extends six wings, each to represent one of the six religions of the world which are international in scope: Hinduism, Judaism, Buddhism, Confucianism, Christianity and Islam." The priesthood which helped create and now operates the Temple is the United Lodge of Theosophists of New York through the tax-exempt Lucis Trust (formerly Lucifer Press).

The Lucis Trust has also maintained the Meditation Room at the UN headquarters. Bereft of any conventional religious symbols, the room's decor is "the story of the descent of the divine into every human life," according to Theosophist writers.[8]

The UN concept of the divine may be understood when it is realized that Mohammed Ramadan, president of the UN's Society for Enlightenment and Transformation, has opened the UN's headquarters to all varieties of "spiritual sages"— mystics, channelers, UFO enthusiasts and so on. He says, "As 'international civil servants' we are here by divine appointment . . . to further this divine service by serving the servers, teaching and inspiring them . . . ."[9]

One of the main vehicles through which religious people are urged to adopt this planetary outlook is the global environmentalist movement which seeks to direct worship to the goddess Gaia.

As Grigg notes,

In 1990, as though an unseen hand had thrown a switch, nearly every segment of the "social justice industry" suddenly redirected its energies away from supporting Marxist insurgencies in the Third World to laboring on behalf of "Gaia!"[10]

One, among a myriad of efforts, was the production of the 1991 book *Earth Prayers from Around the World* . . . "a collection of prayers [which] remind us of [the] universal marriage of matter and spirit. . . . They make it clear that we humans are not here simply as transients waiting for a ticket to somewhere else. The Earth itself *is* Christos, *is* Buddha, *is* Allah, *is* Gaia."[11]

To disseminate such a philosophy, several major steps have been taken.

In the Summer of 1993

The first step was associated with the periodic Parliament of World Religions held in Chicago. In the view of the Theosophical Society's *Quest* quarterly journal, it was a "Theosophical revival, [in as much as] the Theosophical Society had been a major participant in the first such Parliament 100 years before . . . ."[12]

It is significant to note that the primary text for the Chicago Parliament was *Global 2000 Revisited: What Shall We Do?* written by the Rockefeller Brothers Fund director Gerald Barney who also gave the keynote address. In it he issued an oblique ultimatum: Make your religious traditions "sustainable"—or else. (In Barney's stated opinion, Christianity "as it is understood and practiced now" is not sustainable.)[13]

The Parliament ended with the signing by almost every religious representative present of a "Declaration of a Global Ethic" which was composed to "establish an alternative framework for religion *to which people would be held accountable*" (emphasis added).[14]

The document makes it clear that individual freedoms and property rights must be limited by "the common good of the global community." One of the Global Ethics "Irrevocable Directives" is a commitment to a "culture of tolerance" which indicates that religious leaders who preach "intolerance" should be punished by the loss of their congregation.[15]

Into such a climate a charismatic totalitarian leader would fit very nicely!

On October 9, 1993, representatives from seventy-five mainline religious denominations met with U.S. Vice-President Al Gore to create the "National Religious Partnership for the Environment" (NRPE). Al Gore wrote *Earth in the Balance: Ecology and the Human Spirit* in which he espouses the theosophy of Madame Blavatsky in exalting pagan religious systems (including goddess worship) and indicting the Judeo-Christian theology for earth's environmental crisis. The Partnership is a coalition of four component groups: the National Council of Churches, the U.S. Catholic Conference, the Evangelic [sic] Environmental Network and the Consultation on the Environment and Jewish Life. Most of these groups are not accountable to the rank and file of the churches they supposedly represent and are funded by foundations.

Interestingly enough, the Partnership offices are located at the infamous Cathedral of St. John the Divine in New York City, which also houses the offices of the UN Temple of Understanding and the Lindisforne Association, a Luciferian group.

Religious Convictions Attacked by a World Court

The one-world pressure was turned up several notches in mid-1998 when a five-week UN conference was held in Rome for the purpose of negotiating a UN International Criminal Court (ICC).

The goal of the ICC is to be able to exercise the right to prosecute any citizen of any country in the world, thus bypassing national sovereignty. And what sort of crimes would be punishable by the world court?

Along with genocide and other universally recognized crimes, the ICC draft statute specifies crimes such as "enforced pregnancy," "gender persecution" and would criminalize the spanking of children even in a child's home or a private school.

"Enforced pregnancy" is an acknowledged euphemism for abortion, while "gender persecution" would include any politically incorrect references to homosexuality or lesbianism.

The vision of many of the feminists and other drafters of the ICC is for it to have "broad, inherent jurisdiction" free from Security Council oversight, as well as jurisdiction within countries.

If ever approved as proposed, the ICC would prohibit individual nations from enacting legislation against sodomy, homosexuality and abortion. Parents could be criminalized for physically disciplining their own children.[16] Unquestionably, a global politically correct, one-world church is being formed.

That Old Black Magic

The widespread acceptance of the supernatural is a second trend that indicates the development of Mystery Babylon. At a conference in Arrowhead Springs, California, I heard Dr. Charles Malik, former President of the United Nations, cite the revival of paganism and spiritism as one of the most disturbing trends of our day. Interest in witchcraft, the occult, horoscopes and numerous related supernatural topics has mushroomed.

Many magazines, like *McCalls, Esquire* and *TIME*, ran feature articles at the beginning of the 1970s on what then was termed "the occult explosion." Since then movies, books, magazines and encyclopedias of the supernatural abound. Entire bookstores devoted to the occult are not uncommon. Universities regularly offer courses on witchcraft and magic—usually the so-called "white" variety. Myriads of mystical Eastern religions, bizarre and often demonic, have invaded North America and found in most cases an amazing responsiveness.

Sometime ago, I visited a neighbor who was hospitalized in a nearby city. As we sat and chatted I was amazed to see on the lawn of the hospital a young woman engaged in a series of physical gyrations that suggested a form of bizarre worship. I later discovered that her antics were, indeed, acts of worship to an Eastern deity! And this in public—in a "Bible-belt" section of conservative Canada! What was shocking then is becoming common occurrence.

Dr. Keith Bailey, in *Strange Gods*, has documented the proliferation of pagan and New Age religions throughout North America as part of a world revival of such.

The trend is confirmed by a 1998 *USA Today* survey which showed the growth in the percentage of American adults who said they believed New Age religious concepts.

Belief in spiritualism soared from twelve percent in 1976 to fifty-two percent in 1998; in astrology from seventeen percent to thirty-five percent; reincarnation nine percent to twenty-five percent; and fortune-telling from four percent to fourteen percent.[17]

The "Turned On" Crowd

The third trend, the drug epidemic scarcely needs to be documented. The reason for believing it is related to the emergence of a one-world counterfeit church does need to be spelled out however.

In Revelation 9:21, a group of people whom the prophet foresees as experiencing the judgments of God are described as not "[repenting] of their murders, their magic arts, their sexual immorality or their thefts" in spite of God's judgment.

Several years ago, a Canadian evangelist, in a message on the source of the drug problem, pointed out that the word translated "magic arts" ("sorceries" in other translations) in the above reference is significant. It comes from the Greek word *phar-*

makeia which is the word from which we get our English word "pharmacy" or drugstore. It means a drug-related kind of occult worship or black magic.[18]

And Revelation 18, referring to the prostitute's false religious system, charges that "all the nations were deceived by your sorcery"— the same word, *pharmakeia.*

There can be little question that Satan uses hallucinatory drugs to take people to deeper levels of satanic influence and control. An individual for whom I, along with others, had the awesome privilege of obtaining deliverance from deep entanglement in witchcraft and demonic control confirms from personal experience and observation that this is so.

In Conclusion

Brooks Alexander, of Spiritual Counterfeits Project, Inc., sums it up well in his article, "The Coming World Religion."

He points out that one of the startling features of the early stages of the awful period during which the Antichrist is on the scene will be an unprecedented religious unity.

He notes that the apocalyptic vision of John is one of "ultimate totalitarianism, in which political power, economic control, religious worship, occult gnosis, psychic power, and personal charisma will be combined in a unified system of oppression and delusion called 'Mystery Babylon.' "[19]

The realization of such a prediction is well within the realm of the foreseeable at this point.

The pieces of the puzzle continue to come together!

Notes

1 *Signs of the Times*, January 1981, pp. 10–11.

2 Martin, *The Keys of This Blood*, pp. 304–305.

3 *Canadian Ecumenical News*, November/December, 1982, pp. 4–5.

4 *The Christian Beacon*, June 14, 1970, p. 1.

5 Ibid., p. 1.

6 Martin, op. cit., pp. 297–213.

7   Dennis L. Cuddy, *Now Is the Dawning of the New Age New World Order* (Oklahoma City, OK: Hearthstone Publishing, 1991), p. 312, as quoted by William N. Grigg, *Freedom on the Altar: The UN's Crusade Against God and Family* (Appleton, WI: American Opinion Publishing, 1995), p. 159.

8   Eunice S. Layton and Felix Layton, *Theosophy: Key to Understanding* (Wheaton, IL: The Theosophical Publishing House, 1967), pp. 12–13; Cuddy, p. 159.

9   Columnist Lynch, "At UN, Lobbyists Seek to Open World Body to Other Worlds," *Boston Globe*, December 4, 1993, p. 4.

10 Grigg, op. cit., pp. 169–170.

11 Ibid., p. 171.

12 Robert Ellwood, *Theosophy: A Modern Expression of the Wisdom of the Ages* (Madras, India/London, England: Quest Books [The Theosophical Society], 1986), p. 211.

13 David Briggs, "A UN of Religions? Spiritual Leaders Dream of Bringing Peace on Earth," AP wire service, August 16, 1993.

14 Ibid.

15 *The Declaration of a Global Ethic*, distributed at the Parliament of World's Religions, August 28–September 5, 1993, Chicago, IL, p. 1, as quoted in Grigg, *Freedom on the Altar*, p. 189.

16 "Globocop," *The Alberta Report*, June 29, 1998, pp. 24-30.

17 *USA Today*, April 20, 1998, p. A1.

18 1973 Canadian Crusade Evangelism Newsletter, p. 1.

19 Alexander, "The Coming World Religion," *The Christian Reader*, July/August, 1981, p. 5.

PART FOUR

The Climax of the Ages

Other Signs

Birth pangs. They begin at a given point in time, and then, usually gradually, begin to increase in both frequency and intensity until the actual moment of birth occurs.

Nearly 2,000 years ago, Jesus Christ foretold that certain events would occur in the future. He called these events "birth pangs" which would precede His revelation from heaven and the establishment of His kingdom in earth's climactic age.

Let's look at the evidence for believing that this generation is witnessing the onset of those prophesied "birth pangs."

*"When will these things be? And what will be the sign
of your coming, and of the end of the age?"*
—Questions asked Jesus by His disciples

CHAPTER 17

Jesus Predicts Our Future

The time was just two days before Jesus Christ was crucified. The location was outside the temple in Jerusalem.

In the crowd which thronged that special place were Jesus
and His disciples. The disciples, undoubtedly with a sense of
pride, were commenting on the beauty of the building with its
fine stonework and elaborate ornamentations. For though it
could never compare for magnificence with the original Solo-
mon's Temple, still Herod's Temple was a splendid structure.

Suddenly, and totally unexpectedly, Jesus said, "Do you
see all these things? I tell you the truth, not one stone here
will be left on another; every one will be thrown down."

The disciples were astonished and dismayed. Later, they
came to Jesus privately and asked Him three questions:

1. "When will this happen?"

2. "What will be the sign of your coming?"

3. "What will be the sign of the end of the age?"

Jesus' reply is recorded in Matthew 24, Mark 13 and Luke 21. It is called "the Olivet Discourse" because it was uttered on the Mount of Olives. Here is Luke's account of that answer.

He replied: "Watch out that you are not deceived. For many will come in my name, claiming, 'I am he,' and, 'The time is near.' Do not follow them.

When you hear of wars and revolutions, do not be frightened. These things must happen first, but the end will not come right away."

Then he said to them: "Nation will rise against nation, and kingdom against kingdom.

"There will be great earthquakes, famines and pestilences in various places, and fearful events and great signs from heaven.

"But before all this, they will lay hands on you and persecute you. They will deliver you to synagogues and prisons, and you will be brought before kings and governors, and all on account of my name.

"This will result in your being witnesses to them.

"But make up your mind not to worry beforehand how you will defend yourselves.

"For I will give you words and wisdom that none of your adversaries will be able to resist or contradict.

"You will be betrayed even by parents, brothers, relatives and friends, and they will put some of you to death.

"All men will hate you because of me.

"But not a hair of your head will perish.

"By standing firm you will gain life.

"When you see Jerusalem being surrounded by armies, you will know that its desolation is near.

"Then let those who are in Judea flee to the mountains, let those in the city get out, and let those in the country not enter the city.

"For this is the time of punishment in fulfillment of all that has been written.

"How dreadful it will be in those days for pregnant women and nursing mothers! There will be great distress in the land and wrath against this people.

"They will fall by the sword and will be taken as prisoners to all the nations. Jerusalem will be trampled on by the Gentiles until the times of the Gentiles are fulfilled.

"There will be signs in the sun, moon and stars. On the earth, nations will be in anguish and perplexity at the roaring and tossing of the sea.

"Men will faint from terror, apprehensive of what is coming on the world, for the heavenly bodies will be shaken.

"At that time they will see the Son of Man coming in a cloud with power and great glory.

"When these things begin to take place, stand up and lift up your heads, because your redemption is drawing near." (Luke 21:8-28)

These events, according to verse 27, are to be seen as preliminary to the coming of Jesus in a cloud with power and great glory. Jesus called them "birth pangs." That's very significant. For just as a birth is preceded by the pains of birth, which increase in intensity and frequency up to the moment of birth, so these signs—the ones to occur before the appearance of Christ—will be preceded throughout the earth by similar signs or by faint beginnings of the actual signs.

If the revelation of Christ with His saints is indicated by the appearance of these indicators, how much nearer must be the Rapture of the Church which, I believe, precedes the revelation by seven years? (For more detail, see endnote 1.)

Ten Important Indicators

A synopsis of the three accounts of Jesus' prophecy provides us with these ten great indicators of His return:

1. Wars, and as a part of that sign, rumors of wars, commo-

tions, nation rising against nation and kingdom against kingdom.

2. Great earthquakes in various places.

3. Famines.

4. Pestilences.

5. Unusual signs in the heavens, including fearful sights and signs, signs in the sun, moon and stars, with the powers of heaven being shaken.

6. Jerusalem restored to Jewish control after a worldwide dispersion and return to Israel by the Jews.

7. Distress of nations, with perplexity.

8. Men's hearts failing them for fear of what is coming on the earth.

9. False Christs.

10. A worldwide proclamation of the gospel.

That's the list Jesus gave His disciples.

As we set out to see what's happening in our world today in relationship to these indicators, I frankly confess a major problem. There is so much material about each of these that a whole chapter or even an entire book could be written on every one. My problem is to somehow adequately condense these mountains of data into the space available and still do justice to all. That fact indicates as clearly as anything can the rapidity with which developments are occurring.

Let's look at the current birth pangs.

1. Wars and Rumors of Wars

Virtually everyone who has listened regularly to radio or television or who has read the newspapers in recent years has been made aware of seven large-scale wars which have been fought since 1970.

The Vietnam, Falklands, Lebanese, Iran-Iraq, Afghanistan, Gulf and Bosnian wars were truly major conflicts. The 1991 Gulf War also saw the deployment of one of the largest military forces in human history, while the Bosnian War, unspeakably tragic, has seen hundreds of thousands of casualties.

But though one could scarcely escape the fact of these big wars, what few realize is that in the past several decades literally dozens of wars have been going on in scores of nations around the world in addition to these conflicts.

The December 31, 1997, *USA Today* cover story is typical. Headlined "Global Peace Unlikely Prospect in 1998," the article listed ten world hot spots. Adrian Karatucky, president of Freedom House which monitors conflicts, was quoted as saying, "There are 30 to 35 areas where there could be major conflicts [double the conflict zones projected a year earlier]."[2]

Unfortunately, the prediction was quite accurate for 1998—a year filled with internal and external conflict.

Tragically, war has been a way of life in the twentieth century.

Consider just a few of the items I've pulled from my files. *The Chicago Tribune* reported in a news map feature:

> At this moment, in nations scattered throughout the world, 23 major armed conflicts are taking place. More than 8 million soldiers and paramilitary personnel are directly or indirectly involved. . . . As many as 5 million have already been killed. The total number of wounded and maimed could be three times that.[3]

The Economist published a news map of Africa which showed thirty-nine African countries in which a total of 150,785 soldiers from Russia, Cuba, France, Morocco, South Africa, Britain, the U.S., East Germany, Israel, Egypt, Libya, Red China, Belgium, North Korea and several eastern European nations were active in nations other than their own. On that date, five "major conflicts" were in progress.[4]

An article in *The Vancouver Sun* in the mid-1980s contained a news map showing twenty-one wars then raging in countries around the world. Under the heading "Millions Killed in Current Wars" the article reported that the estimates of deaths (prepared by the Washington, DC-based Center for Defense Information) in just ten of those wars totaled 3.76 million!

The authoritative *Jane's Defense Weekly* of London identifies no fewer than seventy-three flashpoints around the globe that threaten regional or international stability, as well as twenty-six wars or insurrections. "We continue to live in the most dangerous decade of the century, and possibly ever," said *Jane's* publisher, Paul Beaver. The same survey identified three concerns that could undermine whole regions: proliferation of ballistic missiles, nuclear weapons and chemical warheads; threats from drug-financed organizations and the movement of refugees.[5]

A *New York Times* news service feature contained a list of forty conflicts then in progress in Europe, Asia, the Middle East, Africa and South America, in which at least 3,600,000 have become casualties.[6]

Of course, there have always been wars throughout human history, but now the tempo and severity of war is rapidly accelerating. In the twentieth century alone we have had over 200 major armed conflicts.

There have been the "big/little" wars: the Russo-Japanese war (1904-05); the Balkan wars (1912-13); the Spanish Civil war (1937-39); the Colombian civil war (1948-53); the Korean war (1950-53); the Vietnam war (1963-73); the Lebanese Civil war (1973-82); the Angolan civil war (1795-1991); the Iran-Iraq war (1980-1988); the Afghanistan civil war (1979-89); the Falklands and Lebanese wars (1982); the Gulf War (1991) and the Bosnian war (1991-1995). In these wars nearly 4 million soldiers and another 1 to 2 million civilians have died.

There have also been the two great World Wars, 1914-18 and 1939-45, in which 10 million and 51 million respectively perished.[7]

The Evangelical Fellowship of Canada publication, *Understanding Our Times*, noted that "[i]n 1986, designated as the United Nations' International Year of Peace, the nations of the world spent $1.2 trillion on weapons—or $2.3 million per minute." The item was headlined, "Unusual Celebration of Peace."[8]

Such expenditures have continued. The World Bank reported world military costs in the 1990s at over $1 trillion per annum.[9]

And the frightful arms race goes on. More and more nations are expected to join the nuclear arms club, with thirty-five projected to possess such arms by the turn of the century. Sixteen nations are known to possess chemical and biological weapons, with another ten thought to possess such and twelve more seeking them.[10] In 1998 both India and Pakistan became nuclear powers.

Awesome new weapons—superkiller subs, planes, chemical and biological arms, neutron bombs and fearful space laser weapons—are being steadily added to the major arsenals of the world. In an article entitled, "How Do You Measure a Trillion Dollars?" Dennis Robertson says that a conservative estimate of the money spent by all nations on national defense since World War II is over $6 trillion![11] The bulk of that has been in recent years, with $1 trillion a year the going rate.

For a person to spend a trillion dollars at the rate of $1 million per day would require that person to live 2.75 centuries, according to Robertson.

And the fear grows when one remembers the chilling observation that "mankind has yet to invent a weapon it has not eventually used."

Since the "end of the Cold War," the production and sale of military hardware has, in fact, diminished scarcely at all with the "U.S. the globe's top weapon merchant" (*TIME*, December 9, 1994, pp. 36–39). The other top arms exporters are Britain, France, Germany, China and Russia. In the case of Russia, great concern has been expressed over not only the safekeeping of its nuclear weapons and fuel, but also the sale of such weapons to nations like Iran and Iraq.

By maintaining the big business which the arms trade unquestionably is, the arms producing and marketing nations are, in the words of Bernard Wood, head of the Organization for Economic Co-operation and Development, "probably suicidal. We are building for ourselves the large-scale problems of tomorrow."[12]

"UN Urged to Combat 'New Global Anarchy' " headlined a Reuters News Agency report. Javier Perez de Cuellar, then UN Secretary General, warned, "We are perilously near to a new international anarchy." He criticized "the current tendency to resort to confrontation, violence and even war" in pursuit of what are seen as vital interests, claims or aspirations. "Such a trend must be reversed before once again we bring upon ourselves a global catastrophe and find ourselves without institutions effective enough to prevent it."[13]

Please note.

Whether or not the "experts" quoted above were or are accurate in their assessments of the future is not really the issue. The fact is that their speculations and pronouncements, right or wrong, constitute "rumors of wars" to go along with the fact of many actual wars.

Wars and rumors of wars, indeed.

Even more significant is the basic meaning of the word "nation" in the phrase "nation shall rise against nation" which Jesus used. The original Greek word translated "nation" is *ethnos*—from which we get our word "ethnic." Race.

I won't even attempt to footnote or document the fact that in recent years ethnic or racial strife has exploded in our world. From the Rodney King riots in Los Angeles to the tragedy in Bosnia (with its racial cleansing—read genocide), to racial violence by Neo-Nazis in Europe, to race warfare in the Indian subcontinent to an estimated 800,000 race-related deaths in Rwanda, Burundi and other African nations—the tragic list seems to go on and on. Your own memory of recent current events tells you that not only in the generally accepted sense is nation against nation, but in the "race against race" sense it is happening on an unprecedented scale.

2. Earthquakes

As with war, earthquakes are not unique to our age. But, like wars, their frequency and severity are dramatically increasing.

A prominent historian of seismology, after nearly a lifetime of study, reckons that major earthquakes have increased in frequency from 137 in the fourteenth century to thousands in our time.[14]

Some years ago, the *World Almanac* reported that thirty-eight of the fifty-seven greatest earthquakes in history have occurred in this century. Another six major quakes that year alone added to the percentage of recent quakes.

A *Gemini News Service* article, "The Age of Disaster," says, "experts warn that we are in the 'age of earthquakes.' "[15]

The *Reader's Digest* article "Where Will the Next Earthquake Strike?" details the fears of seismologists over the "50 percent chance that a major quake [in southern California] will occur within a decade."[16]

Sadly, the reports of earthquakes, with their attendant human suffering and loss of life, are frequent news headlines. My file of news stories on earthquakes is several inches thick.

Since the weekly news feature "Earth Week" began running several years ago each Saturday in newspapers all over the continent, I've been filing them. Though I don't have every one, the reports I do have are revealing in terms of earthquake activity. There has never been a week without at least one earthquake somewhere, and there have been as many as fifteen in a single week all over the globe. The average number of earthquakes worthy of note per week has been 8.56 in the span of the years I've kept track.

According to *News from Israel*, the observatory in Strasbourg, France, which has researched the history of earthquakes, reports were that there were eighty-four earthquakes in the twelfth century. The number has increased to over 2,100 in the nineteenth century.

The total number of earthquakes in the twentieth century will far exceed those of the nineteenth. According to general estimates, in the time span from 1905 to 1975 about 625,700 people lost their lives through earthquakes. From January to July 1976 alone there were 1,015,500 victims of earthquakes! There have been multiplied thousands more since.

A U.S. Geological Survey, Department of the Interior report, reveals that, with one exception (the 1906 San Francisco quake), ten of the strongest U.S. quakes have hit in the last half of the century. Six of these have occurred since 1990.

Some skeptics suggest that there really aren't more earthquakes now—we're just much better at detecting them! Granted, we are better at detecting earthquake activity, but please note the chart carefully. It's been compiled from a 1992 report by Energy, Mines and Resources, Canada, plus news clippings since 1992 (reported in *The Mark of the Beast*, Lalonde and Lalonde, p. 172). And notice: the chart lists only major quakes which haven't needed sophisticated technology for detection!

Earthquakes 6.5 or Greater or Causing Significant Death or Destruction

1900-1969 48 earthquakes	Average: .058 per month	.7 per year
1970-1989 33 earthquakes	Average: .14 per month	16.5 per year
1990-1995 over 150 earthquakes	Average: over 2 per month	25 per year

The beginning of "sorrows"? It very much looks like it.

3. Famines

Though it is difficult to comprehend in affluent North America, where a sizable percentage of the population is overweight and where helping people diet is a major business, there are in our world many places where serious famine is a fact of life—and death.

The list of just the recent major famines is a long and tragic one. China, Bangladesh, Kampuchea, Ethiopia, Somalia and North Korea are places where hundreds of thousands have died.

As many as 200,000 are believed to have perished of famine in Iraq.[17] In Sudan, 1.5 million people have died since 1983, most as a result of politically induced famine.[18] An estimated 350,000 more faced starvation there in late 1998.[19]

It is believed that in North Korea famine conditions which became critical in mid-1995 had, by late 1998, resulted in 2 million deaths, almost one-tenth of the population.[20]

A UN World Food Summit in 1997 revealed that some 800 million of earth's peoples suffer from malnutrition or starvation. In Africa, over ten nations were reported as being either in famine situations or at risk.

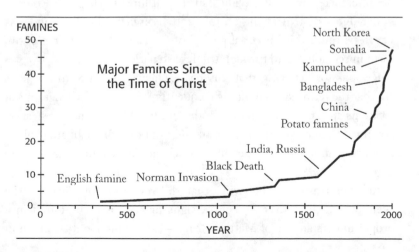

203

The preceding graph[21] of major famines recorded since the time of Christ clearly indicates the almost exponential growth in this tragic human condition, a number of these exacerbated by war or political motivation.

Surprisingly, in a world of remarkable technical advance and agricultural know-how, famine is increasing dramatically. It does appear to be a significant sign.

In Chapter 18 we'll look at the rest of the birth pangs of the climax of the ages.

Notes

1 There are several ways of interpreting this prophecy of Jesus in the Olivet Discourse.

One view says it was all fulfilled in the past and applies only to what has already occurred. The problem with such a view is to explain how Jesus could have already returned at the time of the destruction of Jerusalem!

A second view holds that the prophecy applies to this entire Church age in which we now live, and especially its closing days. Proponents of this view hold that the Church experiences the Tribulation.

A third view, and the one held by this author, *is that the prophecy has exclusive reference to the Jewish nation and Jewish believers.* It also has a double reference, part of it having had its fulfillment when the Romans under Titus destroyed the temple and Jerusalem. The remainder is yet to be fulfilled in the final period of God's dealing with the entire earth in relation to and through the Jewish nation.

Reasons for believing that this has exclusive reference to the Jews are that the term "synagogue" is frequently used; specific geographical locations such as Jerusalem and Judea are mentioned; and the hearers are urged to pray that their flight would not be on the Sabbath—all indicators pointing to the fact that Israel, not the Church, is in view here.

Another reason for believing that the revelation of Christ is the event which the Olivet Discourse signs precede is to be found in a proper understanding of Matthew 24:40–41. It talks about two men in a field: "one will be taken and the other left." This has generally been understood to be a reference to a "taking" in the Rapture. However, the context reveals it to be a "taking" in judgment, since it is the same Greek word as is used in the previous verse where the text speaks of the flood "taking" people away (in judgment). Thus the one who is "taken" in Matthew 24:40–41 is the unrighteous person, who is taken in judgment at the revelation of Christ. The one who is left is one who has become righteous and remains to enter the Millennial kingdom.

The signs of His appearing, prophesied by Jesus Himself, had in many instances a prior fulfillment at Jerusalem's fall in A.D. 70. But while they will be finally and completely fulfilled in the last seven years before the establishment of Christ's kingdom upon earth, they will not burst suddenly upon the world. Rather, they will be preceded by a building toward their complete fulfillment.

In summary, I believe the actual events prophesied by Jesus in Matthew 24, Mark 13 and Luke 21 will occur between the Rapture (when Christ comes in the air for His Church) and the Revelation (when Christ returns to the air with His Church).

2 *USA Today*, December 31, 1997. p. A1.

3 *The Chicago Tribune*, January 11, 1980, p. A3.

4 As reproduced in *The Globe and Mail*, September 26, 1981, p. 9.

5 Reported in *The Patriot News*, Harrisburg, PA, January 3, 1993, p. A11.

6 *The Patriot News*, Harrisburg, PA, February 9, 1993. p. A2.

7 C. Chant, R. Holmes, W. Koenig, eds., *Two Centuries of Warfare* (Hong Kong, Octopus Books, 1978).

8 *The Vancouver Sun*, October 25, 1986, p. B3.

9 *The Patriot News*, Harrisburg, PA, July 8, 1992, p. A8.

10 *OMNI* magazine, May 1991, pp. 44–48, 111–113.

11 *The Plain Truth*, October 1882, p. 7.

12 *The Christian Inquirer*, April 1980, p. 7.

13 *U.S. News & World Report*, May 19, 1980, pp. 23–26.

14 Quoted by Dr. John W. White in *World War III* (Grand Rapids, MI: Zondervan Publishing House, 1977), pp. 46–50.

15 *The Vancouver Sun*, April 8, 1979, p. A5.

16 *The Reader's Digest*, June 1981, pp. 159–166.

17 *Cleveland Plain Dealer*, April 7, 1998, p. A1.

18 *U.S. News & World Report*, September 14, 1998, pp. 38-43.

19 *The Patriot News*, Harrisburg, PA, April 7, 1998, p. A7.

20 *The Sentinel*, Carlisle, PA, August 14, 1998, p. A2.

21 "World Watch AP Research," as reproduced in *Unmasking the Enemy*, p. 373.

CHAPTER 18

More of Earth's Birth Pangs

The list of indicators of earth's impending climax which Jesus revealed nearly 2,000 years ago does not make for light cheerful reading. Yet, since much of it is current news, it is definitely captivating.

In addition to the signs already considered, let's check out the rest of the birth pang signs Jesus listed.

4. Pestilences

A short time ago it was being suggested that technological advances and scientific know-how were going to eliminate disease and pestilence from the earth.

In September 1966, the U.S. Centers for Disease Control (CDC) indicated that the status of diseases may be classified as follows:

1. Diseases eradicated within the United States (bubonic plague, malaria, smallpox, etc.)

2. Diseases almost eradicated (typhoid, infantile paralysis, diphtheria, etc.)

3. Diseases that still are health problems, although technology exists for effective control (syphilis, tuberculosis, uterine cervix cancer, injury, arthritis, breast cancer, gonorrhea, etc.)

4. Diseases where technology is in early developmental stages or nonexistent and where little capability exists for alleviating or preventing health impairment (leukemia and some other neoplasms, some respiratory diseases and strokes).[1]

The outlook in 1966 was quite optimistic.

Not anymore.

The May 29, 1995, issue of *Newsweek* described in graphic fashion the African outbreak of Ebola, the viral disease which kills within nine days by liquefying its victims' internal organs. The article also presented an overview entitled "A World of Viruses" with a map showing the dozens of places literally around the world where some of the better-known and more significant killer viral outbreaks have recently occurred. These include Ebola, Marburg, Junin, Sabia, Oropouche, Yellow Fever, Rift Valley Fever, Machupo, Lassa, Dengue, HIV, HTLV and Hanta (the new East Asian rodent-born virus which has recently appeared in the southwestern U.S.).[2]

It's a truly frightening scene.

The Coming Plague: Newly Emerging Diseases in a World Out of Balance, by Laurie Ganett, is an exhaustive documentation (750 pages in small type) which paints an absolutely terrifying view of "how and why mankind is *losing* the war against infectious disease" (emphasis mine).

A review of the book in *The New York Times* calls it

A frightening vision of the future and a deeply unsettling one . . . a sober, scary book that not only outlines the dangers posed by emerging diseases but also raises serious questions about two centuries worth of Enlightenment beliefs in science and technology and progress.[3]

In addition to those we've listed from the earlier *Newsweek* quote, Ganett documents the emergence or re-emergence of numerous diseases and epidemics. Bolivian Remorragie fever, the Brazilian meningitis epidemic, swine flu, Legionnaire's disease, toxic shock syndrome, the seal plague, malaria, cholera and more.

And she repeatedly cites the disturbing fact that many of the "old" diseases, particularly malaria, have become drug-resistant. Consequently, malaria killed more people in the 1990s than it did in the 1960s. In Africa, malaria mortality in 1993 was at an all-time high.[4]

National Geographic in a feature story recently reported that "each year five million children in the developing world are killed and another four million permanently harmed by just six diseases—including one million malaria victims in that total."[5]

Other diseases such as measles, diphtheria, rheumatic fever, smallpox and tuberculosis have made major comebacks. In 1998 the World Health Organization (WHO) reported tuberculosis claims as many as 3 million lives each year, with it ranking as a major disease in thirteen countries. The WHO has warned that a growing TB epidemic in Russia threatens Europe.[6] Several of these reviving diseases, particularly TB, owe their gains to another fearful pestilence: AIDS. More on that shortly.

Leprosy, cancer, heart disease and stress, as well as "exotic" diseases like bubonic plague (again getting a grip in areas of Asia) and cholera are major factors today. A serious cholera outbreak occurred in Peru in 1991. Fears of epidemics of cholera and intestinal disease in Iraq and Kuwait following the Gulf War were voiced by World Health officials.[7]

According to a report in *Midnight Call*, a drug resistant bacteria known as enterococci, which first surfaced in a New York hospital in 1989 and is now found coast to coast in the U.S., showed up in a Toronto hospital. The bacteria, which can be fatal to persons with a weak immune system, spreads rapidly. Dr. Donald Low, head of microbiology at Mount Sinai and Princess Margaret Hospitals said of its incredible spread throughout the U.S. hospitals, "It's really phenomenal that one organism has been able to do that so quickly."[8]

Sexual Diseases

Then there are the sexually transmittable diseases—nearly two dozen of them, divided into bacterial, viral, protozoan, fungal and ectoparasitic. According to documented information in "The New Silent Epidemic" by D.D. Schroeder, more than twenty of these sexually transmittable diseases are out of control. One of these is viral herpes, for which there is no known cure. *TIME* magazine calls it "the new sexual leprosy."[9] Though dating back to before the Roman Empire, its incidence has, in recent years, exploded as a result of the "sexual revolution." *U.S. News & World Report* calls it "a worldwide epidemic" and reports it is associated with human cancers.[10] A strain of gonorrhea which is "totally penicillin-resistant" has also emerged and become widespread since 1976. Many of the sexual diseases were unknown a decade ago.

AIDS

Most fearful of all, in terms of sexually transmittable diseases is AIDS—acquired immune deficiency syndrome. This incurable fatal ailment was first detected in 1979. The U.S. Public Health Service has designated AIDS its "number one priority."[11]

In an article in *The New American*, entitled "AIDS: A Clear and Present Danger for Civilization," Dr. Paul Cameron suggests that AIDS could wreak unbelievable havoc for all mankind. "The AIDS epidemic will produce an enormous and frightening effect on world health that public health officials may be relatively powerless to contain," says Dr. William Haseltine of Harvard University School of Public Health, as quoted in *The AIDS Cover-Up?*[12]

210

Haseltine also says that the AIDS virus reproduces 1,000 times faster than other viruses and fears the disease may become the world's worst epidemic since the Black Death of the Middle Ages.[13]

Headlining a companion article entitled "You Haven't Heard Anything Yet," *TIME* writers sketched a frightening picture of a growing menace which many authorities fear could become the greatest epidemic ever to come upon the human race.

In Central Africa, according to yet another article in the same issue of *TIME*, there has been a "geometric explosion of the disease" with 5,000 deaths at that date and a "million more at risk."[14]

Newsweek magazine in a feature article recently projected 6 million AIDS deaths, worldwide, by 2000, with 1 million in the U.S. That number is up from the 1985 estimate of a few thousand.[15]

To attempt to be current on the danger of AIDS is virtually impossible. My file of articles and reports on the subject is over a foot thick with new material added weekly. Almost any statistic quoted is outdated as soon as it's in print—usually by more distressing reports and projections.

The words of Kenyan AIDS physician Mboga Okeyo seem to sum it up: "[AIDS] is threatening to clear the world. Africa first. Then India, then Southeast Asia. Then, who knows?"[16]

His gloomy forecast is echoed by scores of serious medical scientists.

Superbugs

Ganett, in her look at the spread of disease globally, makes a strong case for the deadly role played by insects. They're on the march.

A *Parade* magazine article entitled, "Superbugs: A New Biblical Plague?" indicates that insect pestilence is indeed a major problem.

Describing some of the 364 "superbugs" which have become resistant to the poisons developed to destroy or hold them in check, the article calls them "the shock troops of a global insect army locked in constant combat with man, challenging us for our food and fibre supplies and bringing death, disease and discomfort to millions, particularly in Asia, Africa and Latin America."

Viewed in terms of war, it is the insects that are on the offensive. "They are beginning to tip the scales in their favor," warns Dr. Paul Schwartz, a U.S. Department of Agriculture (USDA) entomologist. "The potential for disaster is always present—in agriculture or in disease."

The United Nations Environment Program, in its recent State of the World report, noted with alarm the rapid gains made by insects, mites, ticks, rodents, weeds and fungi in becoming increasingly resistant to pesticides. This poses a grave threat to world health and food production.[17]

Killer bees, fire ants, locust invasions and similar pestilential insects really do appear to be on the march. In recent decades, according to a UPI release from Rome, the threat of an astronomical locust plague is described by UN locust specialist Jean Roy as containing the potential for disaster for Africa and Asia.[18] So severe is the infestation that a missionary from Mali, Africa, recently reported that as many as twelve locusts have been seen attacking a single stock of millet.

Pollution

The pollution of earth's atmosphere and resources is a fearful, though little-understood pestilence. It is apparent no one really knows the long-term effects of hazardous waste and chemical contamination (like Love Canal); the "garbaging" of earth's oceans;[19] the underground contamination of water supplies; the threat of earth's oxygen supply through industrial pollution and the savage destruction of earth's forests such as the Amazon rain forest which is said to supply half the world's oxygen;[20] the awesome acid rain and Arctic haze threat—products of both North American and Soviet industry;[21] or the danger of unknown effects on the earth from the enormous amounts of dust blasted into the atmosphere by volcanic action in the Philippines, the U.S., Mexico and Indonesia. The El Chicon volcano's cloud is said to have blocked five to ten percent of the sun's light in a solid belt around the earth from the equator to Texas.

The effects of the Chernobyl nuclear disaster are still incalculable at this point. Estimates are that its devastating effect on the environment and on mankind will result in multiplied thousands of deaths in the next several decades. Oil spills, like the Exxon Valdez disaster in Alaska, take their toll. The enormous environmental pollution from the deliberate oil spills and torched oil wells during the Gulf War is expected to span decades.

5. Unusual Occurrences in the Heavens

When the term "heavens" is used in Scripture it can have one of three meanings: the atmospheric heavens, the cosmical heavens, home of the heavenly bodies we call planets and stars or the dwelling place of God and the inhabitants of heaven.

The *atmospheric heavens* have unquestionably been the arena of strange occurrences in recent years, with the media full of reports of most unusual weather patterns and other phenomena.

An Associated Press report sums up the situation in these words, under the headline, "Wacky Weather: Scientists Baffled": "Snow in the Middle East. No snow in Quebec. Daffodils in Sweden in winter. India freezes. Moscow warms up."

If you're baffled by the recent topsy-turvy weather, you are not alone. Some of the worlds' top weather scientists freely admit they don't understand what's happening either. Or why.[22]

Record heat waves, droughts, rainfalls, floods, blizzards and cold spells, often in areas where such events have not occurred, are results of the "wacky weather." A *U.S. News & World Report* article asks, "Is Mother Nature Going Ber-

213

serk?"[23] as it reviews the strange occurrences in weather around the world. The debate rages as to whether the world is heading into another ice age or into a wet and warm greenhouse effect period, or a time of unprecedented drought.

In the winter of 1982–83 the world's largest weather system, as the *National Geographic* calls it, the El Niño current off the Peruvian coast of South America, went haywire.

The result was berserk weather around the world. The February 1984 issue of *National Geographic* chronicled the incredible worldwide impact this phenomenon had. According to the report, $8.65 billion dollars of damage was done in Australia, Indonesia, Philippines, India, Sri Lanka, Central America, Mexico, South America, Southern Africa and the U.S. as a result of storms, floods, drought and disruption.

The worst of it, said the report, was the loss of human lives which no accounting can reckon. "Yet the mounting statistics of crops destroyed, livestock killed, of birds and marine life vanished lengthened the ledger of misery . . . created by the century's most destructive El Niño."[24]

But the 1984 El Niño was nothing compared to the 1997-1998 one. Incredible disruptions all over the world resulted in billions of dollars of damage, tremendous loss of human life and enormous harm to the environment and the global economy.

Mitch, history's most devastating hurricane in terms of loss of human life, occurred in October 1998 with the death of up to 20,000 people in Central America. And another stronger-than-normal system, La Niña—the reverse of El Niño—prolongs earth's weather woes in the winter of 1998-1999.

Scientists were warning, in the wake of the record northeast U.S. blizzard in January of 1996, that the paralyzing storm and the resultant floods may be a sign of catastrophic warming. If they are right, future weather will turn really extreme—more floods, worse hurricanes, larger droughts and yes—heat waves. Such shifts would intensify the serious global food shortage as shorter growing seasons, heat waves, widespread drought or repeated floodings in the food-producing areas of the world combine to take their toll.

A UPI release from Geneva quotes the experts convened by the World Meteorological Organization, United Nations Environmental Program and the International Council of Scientific Unions as seeing weather changes "materially affecting food production and water supplies."[25]

UFOs

A phenomenon classifiable as an "unusual occurrence in the heavens" is that of UFOs. An enormous amount of interest in and debate over the existence of Unidentified Flying Objects continues year after year.

The fiftieth anniversary of the alleged crash of a UFO at Roswell, New Mexico in 1947, along with the release of a spate of UFO movies, books and TV shows, generated tremendous interest in the subject in the late 1990s. A bizarre mass suicide in California related to UFO belief dominated the news in early 1997.

While I am convinced that UFOs have prophetic significance, the subject is too broad to get into in this volume. The reader is referred to my book, *UFOs: Friend, Foe or Fantasy?* for an in-depth study of the phenomenon.

Asteroids

A heavenly sign which has grabbed a good deal of attention after comet fragments spectacularly crashed into Jupiter in mid-1994 is the possibility of asteriods striking earth.

There have been some near misses recently. In 1989 an asteroid the size of an aircraft carrier passed through earth's orbit at a point where the planet had been only six hours earlier. In 1991 there was another close call with an asteriod passing by less than half the distance to the moon.

In December 1992, the two-part asteriod Toutasis—one chunk nearly a half-mile wide and the second a bit smaller—

whizzed by a mere 2.2 million miles away. In celestial terms that's a "hair-thin margin of safety." A direct hit, say the experts, would have produced a global disaster in which millions would have perished.[26]

A *Newsweek* feature further explained the concerns. The Planet Crossing Asteriod Survey, coordinated by the Jet Propulsion Lab, is an international program whose orbits cross earth's are called Apollo objects of which NASA reports there are some 4,000 more than half-a-mile wide. Astronomers estimate that about eighty of these are on courses which could lead to collision with earth. Serious commitment to the development of interception and deflection programs is urged by many scientists.

Planets

Another level of heavenly signs is in the planets. The discovery by University of Arizona physicists of fifty-mile-high gas waves on the sun's surface is said to add credence to long-held theories that "fire storms on the face of the sun also affect the earth."[27]

Marsha Adams, of the research firm SRI International, says it is believed that solar-flare activity has an effect on weather, earthquakes, electrical malfunctions, human illness and fatigue, as well as riots, crime sprees and political instability. Increased sun-storm activity is predicted, according to a UPI release.[28]

Meanwhile, other scientists note with concern a dip in solar energy. Physicist Richard Willson of the Jet Propulsion Laboratory, Pasadena, California, in not sure whether the dip is a temporary one or the beginning of long-term trend.[29]

In July 1996, data collected by the SOHO spacecraft during a solar flare provided scientists at Stanford University, Palo Alto, California, and the Glasgow University, Scotland, with the first-ever observation of a sunquake equal to a magnitude 11.3 trembler on the earth. It released 40,000 times the energy of the 7.8 San Francisco quake of 1906.[30]

Whatever the implications of these and other events, the fact remains that, taking the various meanings of the heavens into account, there does appear to be many signs in the heavens in our time.

6. Jerusalem Restored to the Jews

It is a fact of history that Jerusalem was totally lost to the Jews in A.D. 70, at which time the Jews were dispersed worldwide and ceased to exist as a nation.

Until 1967, the city of Jerusalem was controlled either totally or in part by non-Jewish, that is, Gentile people.

However, on June 6, 1967, during the Six-Day War, the Holy City, for the first time in 1,900 years, was returned to Jewish control. Shortly after the capture of Old Jerusalem, and while the war was still raging, the late General Moshe Dayan marched to the Wailing Wall—that last remnant of the Old Temple—and said, "We have returned to our holiest of Holy Places, never to leave again."[31]

Since then, in the face of a great deal of worldwide opposition, the city has been made the capital of the State of Israel, with the seat of government being moved from Tel Aviv and the Hebrew spelling "Jereshulayim" restored.

7. Distress of Nations

The various present-day conditions which have been discussed in this book—inflation, economic concerns, war, famine, pestilence, ecological problems, the rape of irreplaceable resources and many more—are all international problems.

Their enormity is compounded by their almost universal presence. The result is a high degree of concern and distress among the leadership of nation after nation.

The leaders of the U.S., Britain, France, Japan, Italy, Germany and Canada have been meeting periodically over the past decade or more in summit sessions in an effort to address these global problems."[32]

217

However, following these summit meetings, the pronouncements have been invariably gloomy. A Canadian prime minister bitterly described one set of talks as "totally non-productive, a waste of time." So the leaders of the seven most powerful western nations apparently do not have, and cannot seem to discover, solutions to the distressing problems facing the world. Subsequent summits have done little to alter that view. The failure to discover solutions points out the distress the world faces.[33]

8. Fear

International terrorism in recent years has seen thousands of individuals brutally murdered. It has created a climate of fear that seems to be a symptom of our times.

The New York City World Trade Towers bombing, the Federal Building bombing in Oklahoma City, bombings in Paris' subways, poison gas attacks in Tokyo's subways and many similar incidents around the world create a depressing climate of fear.

In November 1995, terrorist threats forced mission executives to withdraw 130 missionaries from Colombia, South America.

On another level, fear grows over the frequency with which disgruntled fired employees return to their former place of business to kill or wound as many as two dozen people, or the bizarre copycat crimes of torching subway ticket booths or carjacking vehicles at traffic lights. The recent rash of senseless mass killings by school children has created a dreadful climate of fear.

The list seems endless, but the net effect is an atmosphere of fear. A 1994 survey, reported by the Canadian Press, revealed that fewer than three in ten Canadians felt safe on the streets at night.

Providing security for the leaders of nations, prominent businessmen, artists or athletes has become a big business.

The fear is not unfounded. With the appeal of Saddam Hussein, during the 1991 Gulf War, to all Arabs to join a holy war of global terrorism, the threat is very much alive. It is being taken seriously by leaders around the world.

But it is not just the prominent who fear. In the U.S., violence was once described by former Surgeon General C. Everett Koop as the number one health problem. Murders, suicides, rapes, muggings and related violence have created unprecedented fear in major U.S. cities and suburbs, in particular.[34] Elsewhere, too. A *U.S. News &World Report* article on violence is headlined, "Abroad, Too, Fear Grips the Cities."[35]

Fear of being poisoned by radon emissions, pesticides, radiation from computers and TVs, leaded paint and other commonplace items is widespread throughout America, according to *U.S. News & World Report*.

Jean Lawrence, publisher of a Washington, DC newsletter for professional communicators, graphically describes the fear many feel in these words.

> Almost overnight, the world has become a frightening, uncertain place. . . . Businesses, consumers, manufacturers—we're all like jacklighted deer, pinned in place by the horror of war, the ruin of our monetary system, the financial collapse of our cities and the violence in our streets.[36]

Unquestionably, fear stalks the earth.

9. False Christs

The date was April 25, 1982. On that day, full-page advertisements proclaiming that "The Christ is Now Here" appeared in *The New York Times, The Los Angeles Times* and major newspapers in thirty other cities of the world. The ad said that "The World Teacher, Lord Maitreya, known by Christians as Christ, the Jews as the Messiah, Buddhists as the

Fifth Buddha, Moslems as the Iman Mahdi and the Hindus as Krishna—all names for one individual—has been in the world literally since 1977." According to the ad, acknowledgment of the Christ's identity would be made within two months of the publishing of the notice. This would be done through a worldwide television and radio broadcast and his message would also be "heard inwardly, telepathically, by all people in their own language."

No such acknowledgment was ever made,[37] but Benjamin Creme, the chief spokesman for those responsible for the ad, continues to claim that when conditions are right "The Christ" will appear.

Apparently, the feeling is that the conditions are right, or nearly so, for on January 12, 1987, the Tara Center with which Creme is associated, ran a full-page ad in *USA Today*. Headed "The Christ is in The World," the ad said that "we will see him at the earliest possible moment." According to Creme (as declared in numerous media interviews), the Christ is now living in London, has been frequently in contact with Creme and is awaiting the right time for his "manifestation to the world."

Obviously, the financial resources and clout sufficient to place full-page ads in major world-class papers sets this particular claim apart. In other senses, however, this "Christ" is only one of a number of false Christs who have been legion in recent years.

Creme was back in the news in November 1995, claiming that mankind has entered the "era of miracles" as a preparation for Maitreya to reveal himself through global television. Creme cited the September 1995 reports of "milk-drinking Hindu statues" as an example of the new miracles.[38]

Jim Jones, the fanatical false savior who led or forced over 900 people to commit mass suicide at the People's Temple in Guyana in November 1978, was another.

In the mid-1980s, the Bhagwan Shree Rajneesh attracted

some 350,000 disciples worldwide and created a stir when he was ejected from the U.S. in 1986 after the development in Oregon of the largest of his 550 communes. Freewheeling sexual encounters, the ownership of nearly 100 Rolls-Royces (gifts from his disciples), worship from his followers and other bizarre trappings characterized this god.[39] He has since died in India.

Rev. Sun Myung Moon came upon the American scene from Korea in 1972, claiming to be the Messiah. Using extremely questionable methods, he has attracted a large following for his controversial Unification Church. In 1982 he was convicted of tax, immigration and charity violations. Nonetheless, he is another of the present-day "Christs," still active in the mid-1990s, having married 360,000 couples in a worldwide simultaneous ceremony in 1995!

Another god who has had a great impact is His Holiness Maharishi Mahesh Yogi, the creator of the worldwide Transcendental Meditation movement. On several occasions full-page ads inviting national governments to "solve their problems" through contact with the Yogi's World Government of the Age of Enlightenment have appeared throughout the world in many leading news magazines such as *TIME* and *Newsweek*.[40]

In 1994 and late 1995, a total of sixty-nine members of the Order of the Solar Temple cult committed suicide or were murdered in three locations.

The mass suicide of thirty-nine members of a UFO cult in California in 1997 was, in part, based on an acceptance of the godhood of the leader.

"Send Us a Man"

The search for a savior will intensify. As the apparently insoluble problems multiply and become increasingly severe, the inherent desire for a savior, any savior, will grow.

If a man like Paul Henri Spaak, a former Secretary General of NATO and former Prime Minister of Belgium could be quoted as saying, "Send us a man [who can hold the allegiance of all people] and be he god or devil, we will receive him," will not others echo his sentiments?[41] The desire for such a man will have its culmination first in the Antichrist but, after his defeat, in the Lord Jesus Christ who will indeed reign forever and ever.

10. Worldwide Proclamation of the Gospel

The Matthew account of Christ's answer to His disciples' questions about the timing of His return contains what many believe to be a particularly significant sign.

In Matthew 24:14, Jesus said, "And this gospel of the kingdom will be preached in the whole world as a testimony to all nations, and then the end will come."

There are several views held by prophetic students concerning this sign. One view suggests that before Christ will return for His Church the gospel must be proclaimed to all nations. This view has proven to be a great impetus to missions.

Another view holds that this global preaching will be done by a group of 144,000 Jewish evangelists protected from harm by God in order to proclaim the gospel during the Tribulation period after the Church has been taken away.

Those who hold this view also point to the proclamation of the Two Witnesses described in Revelation 11, and of the angel who, according to Revelation 14:6–7, preaches the everlasting gospel to "every nation, tribe, language and people."

Regardless of the view held, however (and proponents of each view can make a good case for their position), it is most significant that some unusual and very major developments are taking place right now in terms of global missionary effort.

In recent years, groups like Operation Mobilization, Youth With a Mission, and World Literature Crusade (with its Every Home Crusade) have stimulated a renewed thrust in missions. Campus Crusade for Christ, with over 14,000 on staff, is seeking to give the gospel to the world through showing the *Jesus* film in scores of nations. Scripture translation and distribution is at a record level, with organizations like The International Bible Society and the Bible League having an impact. Many missionary groups and denominations have set goals for vastly expanded outreach.

In 1978, the U.S. Center for World Mission was created. This interdenominational effort, which envisions the establishment of sister Centers for World Mission around the world, has as its stated goal the preaching of the gospel in the world's 16,500 cultures in which no Christian church exists. The Center, in its brief lifespan, has identified these groups and begun to enunciate studies and strategies to reach them. National Centers for World Mission have emerged as spinoffs.

Consultations on World Evangelization, beginning with the one called by Billy Graham in the early 1970s, have been held periodically, stimulating interest in unreached frontiers and the accomplishment of the global task of telling the world of Christ.

The possibility of the Word of God being preached in all the world even prior to the efforts of the 144,000 sealed ones is very real—especially when radio, gospel recordings, films and satellite TV to even remote villages and areas with gospel dish receivers are taken into consideration. The worldwide Internet is another mind-boggling avenue of gospel proclamation.

To many observers these events reveal that, whether the preaching of the gospel is to be completely fulfilled before or after the Rapture, the evidence of it is being seen all around the world.

Yes, planet earth is running out of time. The indicators which precede the final fulfillment are piling up.

Daniel's Unique Word

In Daniel 12:4, an intriguing prophecy is recorded, in the

context of end-time events: "But you, Daniel, close up and seal the words of the scroll until the time of the end. Many will go here and there to increase knowledge."

Bible scholars generally agree that this prophecy is a clear statement about the time of the end in which the events predicted throughout Daniel's writings would occur. According to the prophecy, the time of the end will be characterized by extensive travel and by an explosive expansion of knowledge.

Without going into great detail, it should be obvious to even the most casual observer that these two conditions are uniquely characteristic of our era.

This generation has seen mankind move from the early days of the automobile to space travel, with the development of a whole new travel industry to care for the needs of earth's globe-trotters.

So far as the increase of knowledge is concerned, an incredible knowledge explosion is underway, exponentially increased by the advent of the computer, interactive TV and, of course, the Internet. More than seventy-five percent of all scientists who have ever lived throughout human history are alive and active today.[42]

Futurist Alvin Toffler in his book, *The Third Wave*, divides history into three waves: the agricultural, the industrial and a rising Third Wave which is driven by computer technology that is transforming the way most of the world lives and thinks into a world of "info-spheres," "techno-spheres," "bio-spheres" and "psycho-spheres."[43]

Without doubt, this age is witnessing a tremendous increase in travel and knowledge. The fulfillment of these prophecies of Daniel just by themselves would not be too conclusive, but when they combine with the many other signs of fulfillment which we've been considering, they become yet another important piece of the prophetic puzzle falling into place.

In Summary

Taken all together, the affairs of this period in human history have to be viewed as being, at the very least, the beginning of the birth pangs of earth's climactic final events!

Notes

1 L. Ganett, *The Coming Plague* (New York: Penguin Books, 1994), p. 32.

2 "A World of Viruses," *Newsweek*, May 29, 1995, pp. 32.

3 L. Ganett, *The Coming Plague*, back cover copy.

4 Ibid., p. 493.

5 *National Geographic*, February 1984, pp. 18–39.

6 *The Patriot News*, October 21, 1997, p. A7.

7 *USA Today*, February 28, 1991, p. 2A.

8 *Midnight Call*, December 1995, p. 11.

9 *TIME*, July 29, 1980, p. 58.

10 *U.S. News & World Report*, August 2, 1980, p.61.

11 "AIDS: A Plague of Fear," *Discover*, July 1983, pp. 28–29.

12 Gene Antonio, *The AIDS Cover-Up?* (San Francisco, CA: Ignatius Press, 1986), foreword.

13 Don Stanton, *Megatrends* (Secunderabad & Perth, Maranatha Revival Crusade, 1985) p. 20.

14 *USA Today*, November 6, 1986, pp. A1–2.

15 *Newsweek*, June 25, 1990, pp. 20-23.

16 As quoted in *The Coming Plague*, p. 238.

17 "The Sunday Observer," *Parade*, September 30, 1979, pp. 4-6.

18 Ibid.

19 *TIME*, January 14, 1991, p. 57.

20 *National Geographic*, February 1984, pp. 18–39.

21 *USA Today*, February 28, 1991, p. 2A.

22 G. Utting, "Wacky Weather," *The Province*, January 18, 1983, p. B3.

23 *U.S. News & World Report*, February 22, 1983, pp. 66–69.

24 *National Geographic*, February 1984, pp. 18–39.

25 *The Los Angeles Times*, August 17, 1983, p. 18.

26 *The Leader Post*, Regina, SK, September 17, 1994, pp. A1-2.

27 *The Province*, January 19, 1982, p. B8.

28 *The State*, May 28, 1998, p. A14.

29 *The Province*, June 28, 1981, p. B1.

30 *Midnight Call*, October 1998, p. 28.

31 As quoted in *The Beginning of the End*, p. 54.

32 *The Province*, January 14, 1983, p. A3.

33 *The Province*, April 21, 1982, p. A3.

34 *The Province*, October 27, 1982, p. A10.

35 *U.S. News & World Report*, February 23, 1981, p. 65.

36 Jean Lawrence, "Cheap Relief," quoted in *Print & Graphics*, March 1991, p. 50.

37 *The Vancouver Sun*, April 25, 1982, p. A12.

38 *The Emergence*, Vol. XIII, No. 9, November 1995.

39 *The Vancouver Sun*, July 16, 1986, p. A10.

40 *U.S. News & World Report*, August 28, 1983, p. 68.

41 P.H. Spaak quoted in *Moody Monthly*, March 1974, p. 43.

42 J.W. White, *World War III*, pp. 31-38.

43 Alvin Toffler, *The Third Wave* (New York: Morrow, 1980), cover.

The Climax of the Ages

Putting It All Together

What will it be like in a brave new world such as the one described by the ancient biblical prophecies?

While no one can predict with accuracy the details of life under the coming world ruler, the broad principles of the prophetic writings—coupled with current trends—do enable us to have some informed idea of what may occur.

Part Five presents a possible scenario of one person's life in the perhaps not-too-distant future.

CHAPTER 19

A Day in the Life—"Restored Order"

Marianna was deeply depressed. It was her twenty-eighth birthday, but it wasn't a joyous one. So many disturbing things had happened in the past few years that there were no sunny days, no happy smiles, no cause for anything but despair.

The worst event had been her involuntary separation from her family and her enforced move from Pennsylvania to Montana—under the authority of Executive Order Numbers 11000, 11002 and 11004.

Marianna thought back over the recent traumatic events, all of which had happened so quickly, one right on top of the other, it seemed.

First, she recalled that a great many people—hundreds of thousands around the world—had gone missing, including her friend Jenna. They were the "Christian crowd," derisively dubbed so by the media which had happily bid them good riddance.

Marianna remembered how an elderly Barbara Manx Hubbard, New Age author and one-time candidate for a major party vice-presidential nomination, had appeared on *20/20* to shed light on the mysterious disappearances. She had explained that the missing ones had been removed from earth by the Ascended Masters because they were divisive and were holding back the move of mankind toward a one-world society. They would be reprogrammed elsewhere, she said, and if responsive could possibly be returned to share in the coming glorious future.[1]

The disfavor into which Christians had fallen in the U.S. in the late 1980s and 1990s had made many people glad that they were gone, however it had happened. They'd been considered narrow hate-mongers, holier-than-thou prudes with their anti-abortion, anti-gay, anti-sexual-freedom rantings.

Besides, Christians had been persecuted, enslaved, even killed by the thousands around the world in the last half of the twentieth century.

Marianna's thoughts shifted to her own desperate financial plight. She recalled the downward spiral that had brought her to this point. The economic downturn that had started in Thailand in 1997 had come to a climax shortly after January 1, 2000 when the global Y2K computer-related problems had triggered a massive worldwide recession. Worse, it had been coupled with galloping inflation.

The result was the "mother of all stagflations"—economic stagnation plus inflation—the dread condition which the Federal Reserve Chairman Alan Greenspan had warned about back in July 1998.[2]

Marianna didn't understand it in economic terminology, but she was painfully aware that, even though there had been layoffs, reduced hours and a salary cut at work, the price of everything was still rising rapidly. She noticed it particularly at the checkout counter in the supermarket.

The response to the crises had been the suspension of constitutional rights and the implementation of Executive Orders or Orders in Council in nation after nation.

Around the globe, virtual dictatorships had sprung up overnight in an effort to deal with the world emergency.

It had been a replay, magnified a thousandfold, of the same means by which Germany in the late 1920s had been converted by Hitler from a republic into a Nazi dictatorship in just three months.[3]

Marianna remembered some of the terrible stories which her great grandmother Maria had told her about living in Germany then—the destruction of the economy and its rebuilding into the war machine that created World War II with all of its horror, including the Holocaust that killed 6 million Jews.

Momentarily dismissing the past, Marianna recalled how U.S. Executive Order 10555 had given the President the power to take over all communications media: radio, television, newspapers, magazines, CB, HAM, shortwave, telephone, satellite and the Internet. Other Executive Orders had enabled the government to control utilities, food distribution and farm production, while still others had made possible government control of transportation, including private cars, highways, waterways, railways and airports.

Then, in a strange and inexplicable turn of events that Marianna did not even begin to understand, the President had transferred his national control to that of the brilliant new President of the European Union, John Christobaal. His uncanny and mind-boggling solutions to global problems had earned him the admiration of the entire world.

About that same time, the International Criminal Court, introduced by the United Nations in 1997, the World Parliament of Religions, the ISO9000 Standards Commission, the Global Health, Education and Family Life Commissions, backed by what once was the United Nations' military, had all come together to rapidly take control of human life and activity on a worldwide scale. Thanks to the implanted biometric ID micro-chips, personal freedom and privacy were completely gone.

The ID microchips had been speedily integrated into the new generation of supercomputers which had been unveiled by IBM in 1998, so that all personal behavior and business activity could be monitored.

Marianna remembered how the New Age idea of the god-hood of man had been so widely and quickly accepted, par-ticularly after the Christians went missing. But, she reflected, though everyone was equally a god, some gods, it seemed, were greater and more powerful than others.

And no one was more godlike than Christobaal, President of the World. In fact, as the architect of the recovery from the year 2000 chaos, he was deemed worthy of worship—in an official way, of course.

So the order had come down, followed quickly by its im-plementation, to acknowledge Christobaal's surpassing deity. It was decreed that the ID of every person in the world have added to it his prefix: 666— the number of his name. With-out it, no one could access a bank account, get a driver's li-cense, purchase food or other goods, conduct any legal or commercial business, including buying or selling a house.

Marianna didn't like it.

But what choice did she have?

There was absolutely nothing she could do.

She remembered how she had gently mocked the warnings and invitations of her Christian friend who'd disappeared with all the rest. Now she seemed to be trapped in an increasingly terrifying world in which violence, fear, natural disasters and supernatural dangers increased by the week. Some of the recent cataclysmic storms and asteroid strikes, with their devastating effect on the environment, had been unprecedented in history.

Suddenly, Marianna's stoic resolve crumpled under the weight of her thoughts and she gave way to a flood of de-spairing tears . . . there was no hope.

It's Fiction, Isn't It?

Yes, the scenario sketched above is indeed fictitious.

But, on the basis of what we've considered in the preceding chapters, you must admit: Something like the above is plausible and possible.

Whether the climax of earth's final human government will unfold even remotely in the way we've envisioned is unknown. Particularly uncertain is the suggestion that Y2K could be the event which becomes the catalyst for all the rest.

But the fact remains: The prophetic Scriptures do predict a terrible time of total control by the evil second person of the counterfeit trinity —the Antichrist.

Someday economic conditions *will* be ripe for such control.

That control will be a supernatural one based upon economic coercion. Yes, the economy to come will make possible the diabolical rule of earth's last dictator.

Common sense and true wisdom decree that an existence under his reign should be avoided at all costs.

It can be.

There is a place of security. Read on in Part Six to get directions.

Notes

1 The hypothetical TV interview with Hubbard is based on her commentary on *The Book of Revelation*, written, she claims, with the aid of her spirit guides, as cited by Peter Lalonde in *The Omega Letter*.

2 *US News & World Report*, August 3, 1998, p. 48.

3 John Loeffler, "Three Threats to Freedom," *Personal Update*, March 1998, pp. 8-11.

PART SIX

The Climax of the Ages

The Sign of Safety

Safety! It's one of mankind's most basic needs and desires.

But only those who have lived through a grave threat to life can fully appreciate the wonder of receiving a sign or indication that a place of safety is at hand.

Amidst the dreadful signs of this dark period in human history—signs which point to an awesome climax of earth's ages—is another sign.

It's the sign of safety.

It points to a safety that is for real.

Bona fide.

Believable.

And available.

*"A man will be like a shelter from the wind
and a refuge from the storm."*

—The prophet Isaiah

CHAPTER 20

The Only Sure Shelter

As a child, I was very keenly interested in the work of E.J. Pace, a gospel cartoonist, whose pen-and-ink drawings were extremely popular at the time. The artist's skill was matched by his ability to "cartoon" biblical truths in an understandable and graphic fashion.

One of his cartoons which made a vivid impression upon my childish mind and which I can still visualize clearly some decades later had to do with a place of safety in a storm.

In this cartoon, Pace depicted a fearful, tornado-like storm sweeping across the distant land. In the foreground were people—men, women, children and teens—running as fast as they could toward a huge outcropping of rock. Under the overhang and in the crevices of the rock were people who had already reached safety. The rock resembled the head of Jesus Christ as artists depict Him.

The caption read, "A man will be like a shelter from the wind and a refuge from the storm" (Isaiah 32:2), followed by the words—"The Only Place of Safety."

The truth of that old cartoon is more valid than ever today. An awesome storm of end-time events is brooding over the world. Those ominous clouds represent the scenario we have been considering: the Antichrist's diabolical reign; the horror of a world gone mad with sin, hatred, violence and lust; and the terror of a planet reeling under the righteous judgments of a holy but justly wrathful God.

To fully appreciate how terrible this impending storm will be, read carefully the last book of the New Testament, the book of Revelation, particularly Chapters 6 through 20. There has never been in all of human history a storm to rival this one!

There is only one sure place of safety from that storm. That hiding place is a Person, the Lord Jesus Christ.

Perhaps you have experienced what it is to place your confidence in a thing or person only to be disillusioned. Not every refuge is secure. The good news is that Jesus Christ can be trusted. His claims to deity can be depended upon completely.

It was the famed British writer C.S. Lewis who suggested the following argument in support of the claims of Christ: There are only four possible conclusions a thinking person can come to concerning Jesus Christ. He's either a liar, a lunatic, a legend or Lord! In the light of the claims He made about Himself and the things the prophets said of Him, He has to be one of these four.

Consider: If He knew the claims He made were not true, but He made them anyway, then, of course, He was a liar.

If He believed His claims, but they weren't true, then He was deluded and nothing short of a lunatic.

If He didn't make the claims attributed to Him, but they were simply the work of an enthusiastic but misguided band of followers, then He is merely a legend.

The truth is that history gives the lie to each of these options about Jesus Christ. The only logical conclusion a thinking person can come to is that He is who He claimed to be—the Lord Jesus Christ.

He, and He alone, is worthy to be Lord!

History also supports Christ's claims. Dr. Peter Stoner, in his fascinating book, *Science Speaks*, applies the test of the science of probability to the prophecies concerning Jesus Christ. His conclusion is that fulfilled prophecy, as it relates to Jesus Christ and as it is documented in history, is a conclusive demonstration of His authenticity and deity.

He is who He claimed to be—the divine Son of God and only Savior.

As such, He alone can be a place of safety.

Knowing Christ personally is more than just a spiritual exercise. Salvation, while providing safety for eternity, is also very practical here and now on earth.

A Person *a Hiding Place?*

But how can a *Person* be a hiding place?

How does one go about hiding in Christ?

The answer to the first question is that safety comes when a person places his or her hope for salvation in Christ and is forgiven, cleansed, born again—and becomes a member of God's family.

The Bible says that "He [Jesus Christ] is able to guard what I have entrusted to him for that day [the future]" (2 Timothy 1:12). And "[God] who began a good work in you will carry it on to completion until the day of Christ Jesus" (Philippians 1:6).

We are *His* responsibility.

To answer the second question, "How does one go about hiding in Christ?", let me explain the "ABC Steps." ABC stands for:

1. Agree

2. Believe

3. Call

First: Agree

Agree with God that you are separated from Him by your sins, that you have broken His righteous laws.

Agree with God that sin deserves punishment because He is a just, holy and righteous God.

The Bible says:

> [F]or all have sinned and fall short of the glory [the standard] of God. (Romans 3:23)

> Your [the Lord's] eyes are too pure to look on evil; you cannot tolerate wrong. (Habakkuk 1:13)

> Nothing impure will ever enter it [heaven], nor will anyone who does what is shameful or deceitful. (Revelation 21:27)

> All wrongdoing is sin. (1 John 5:17)

> For the wages of sin is death. (Romans 6:23)

The Bible describes three kinds of death: *physical* death (the state experienced when life leaves our bodies); *spiritual* death (spiritual separation from a holy God caused by our sin—a person can be alive physically but dead spiritually, Ephesians 2:1); and *eternal* death (the fixed state entered by the individual who dies physically while he is still dead spiritually).

Eternal death is the result or "wages" of sin. Jesus frequently described such death as being without end in a destiny which He called hell (Matthew 13:42, 50; 18:8; 24:51; Luke 16:24-25, 28; Mark 9:44;). In fact, Jesus more often warned about hell than He spoke about heaven. It is not God's will that any person should perish in hell (2 Peter 3:9), but rather that all should come to repentance.

Agreeing with God, then, about your sin and your need of a Savior is the first step of the ABCs of salvation.

Second: Believe

Believe that God does not want you to perish eternally.

Believe that you cannot save yourself from such punishment.

Believe that God loves you so much that He provided a way to pardon you.

Believe that God sent His only begotten Son—the Lord Jesus Christ—to earth to personally pay for your sin.

Believe that He rose again and ascended to heaven.

Believe that He wants to save you and that He will save you:

> The Lord . . . is patient with you, not wanting anyone to perish, but everyone to come to repentance. (2 Peter 3:9)

> For God so loved the world that he gave his one and only Son that whoever believes in him shall not perish but have eternal life. (John 3:16)

> But God demonstrates his own love for us in this: While we were still sinners, Christ died for us. (Romans 5:8)

> Salvation is found in no one else, for there is no other name under heaven given to men by which we must be saved. (Acts 4:12)

> Jesus answered, "I am the way and the truth and the life. No one comes to the Father except through me." (John 14:6)

Third: Call

How do you call?

Calling is just another term for praying or talking to God. To talk to God is not a complicated process dependent upon some special rituals. God invites people to approach Him in simple, straightforward terms.

While the exact words of your prayer are not important (since God sees and knows the attitude of your heart), the following is a kind of pattern prayer that you could use to call upon God for salvation:

Dear Lord Jesus:
I realize that I need You. I admit that I have sinned and that I deserve punishment for that sin. But I am sorry for my sin and willing to turn from it. I believe that You died and rose again to pay sin's penalty on my behalf. I come to You now and open my heart to You. I ask You to come into my life, forgive me for all my sin, cleanse me from it and make me Your child. I invite You to take control of my life and to cause me to be the kind of person that You want me to be. And I thank You for doing this, because You have promised that whoever calls upon You, as I have done now, shall be saved. Amen.

If this prayer expresses the desire of your heart, I urge you to express it to God as your own prayer, in the name of His Son, Jesus Christ.

Everyone who calls on the name of the Lord will be saved. (Romans 10:13)

. . . the gift of God is eternal life in Christ Jesus our Lord. (Romans 6:23)

Now that you have received Christ into your life and are a part of God's family, follow up your decision by reading and memorizing His Word (1 Peter 2:2). Talk to the Lord. Share with Him your desires, needs, burdens and blessings. Invite Him to control and direct your life (Ephesians 5:18).

Look for the family of God in a local church where the pastor and people believe and teach the Bible. Make a practice of attending such a church (Hebrews 10:24-25) and talk to the pastor about what the Bible says about obedience to Christ in baptism and how to grow as a Christian.

Jesus told His disciples to watch for His return (Matthew

24:42) and to serve Him until He comes (Luke 19:13). The apostle John adds that "everyone who has this hope in him purifies himself, just as he [Christ] is pure" (1 John 3:3).

May you—and all of us who know Him—live in such a way until He comes.

Maranatha! The Lord is coming!

APPENDIX A

Prophets

Those ancient Hebrew prophets who have given us the detailed prophecies were men who had to be willing to stake their very lives on the absolute truth of their prophetic messages.

Here's how.

The Acid Test

Israel's great deliverer and leader, Moses, confirmed that through the course of the nation's history many prophets would come to declare God's Word to the Jewish people. Someone asked at that point how the nation could "know the word which God has not spoken"—i.e., how the Jewish people could decide what was God's message and what was simply the word of the human messenger.

Moses' answer, recorded in Deuteronomy 18:22 (KJV), was simple. It is the acid test of a true prophet: "When a prophet speaketh in the name of the LORD, if the thing follow not, nor come to pass, that is the thing which the LORD hath not spoken."[1]

The penalty, under Jewish law, for falsely claiming to be a prophet was death—capital punishment by stoning.

Even under such harsh conditions, however, many of the biblical prophets made short-term prophecies which could be, and were, fulfilled in their lifetimes. Obviously, they were for real.

Others gave long-range prophecies or prophecies which undoubtedly had a double reference, that is, both a short- and long-term meaning. Many such prophecies, especially those about the Messiah, had short-term references to Christ's first appearance on earth (already fulfilled and documented by history) as well as long-term references to His second coming.

Frequently, the prophets did not themselves understand the significance of their own utterances, as the apostle Peter points out in his New Testament book, Second Peter.

To be valid, a prophecy must be of such a nature that the one who utters it cannot influence its fulfillment—prevented either by time or circumstances from interfering in its outcome. It must also be in such sufficient detail that it can't have numerous possible meanings which would enable the prophet to explain away an apparent failure.

Fantastic Feats of Forecasting

The Hebrew prophets, whose utterances (given as long as 4,000 years ago) have been preserved for us in the Bible, clearly meet all of these criteria.

Isaiah Is Right On

For example, Isaiah prophesied over a span of about sixty years during the reign of four successive kings of Judah. His authenticity as a bona fide spokesman for God, when submitted to Moses' acid test, was demonstrated time and again.

During the reign of Hezekiah (circa 710 B.C.), the mighty Assyrian army led by the cruel King Sennacherib invaded and besieged Jerusalem. As recorded in Isaiah 37:33-38, the prophet made a short-term prophecy that, contrary to Sennacherib's plans and threats, he would not attack Jerusalem but would return to his own land.

History records that it happened as the prophet said. When a rumor of internal problems at home reached Sennacherib, he abandoned the siege, returned home and was assassinated, with his own sons doing the dastardly deed!

Isaiah also made long-range predictions.

In chapter 39:5-7, he predicted that Babylon would destroy Judah and carry away all the treasures of Israel, with the surviving sons of royalty becoming eunuchs in Babylon. Just over a hundred years later, in 586 B.C., this prediction came to pass.

Then, as recorded in Isaiah 13:17-22, the prophet foretold that the seemingly invincible Babylonian Empire would be conquered and the city of Babylon so completely destroyed that it would be uninhabitable. That prophecy really put Isaiah out on a limb, for at the time it was uttered Babylon was considered to be an impregnable city with walls 150 feet high and so thick that five chariots abreast could drive on top of them. The city, one of the seven wonders of the ancient world, was also so self-sustaining that it was thought to be impervious to siege.

But in 539 B.C., approximately 150 years after Isaiah prophesied, Babylon fell to the Medes and Persians. Ultimately, the city sank into ruin from which it has never recovered. (Iraq, however, prior to the Gulf War, attempted to rebuild and revive the ancient capital as part of a plan to make Saddam Hussein a second Nebuchadnezzar.)

Again, Isaiah prophesied that a king whom he actually named—Cyrus—would make possible the rebuilding of Jerusalem and the temple by allowing the Jewish captives to return to Palestine for this work. The prophecy is recorded in Isaiah 44:28 to 45:4. Two hundred years later the Persian King Cyrus allowed the Jewish exiles remaining from the Babylonian captivity to return to Jerusalem for the work of reconstruction, even providing requisitions for materials!

It's quite an impressive record for Isaiah—if he was just

guessing. A most unlikely short-term prophecy was right on; it was followed by three completely accurate long-term forecasts involving 100, 150 and 200 year spans. And these are only four of numerous prophetic utterances by Isaiah! Only divine revelation can explain such feats of foresight.

Some scholars who would like to explain away the miracle of prophecy have charged that Isaiah lived later in history than claimed. Their "late dating" of Isaiah implies that he wrote his so-called prophecies after they actually happened, making him a fraud.

But such a charge makes more than Isaiah a fraud. It also makes frauds and charlatans of the Jewish people who have retained for posterity Isaiah's writings as genuine and whose Museum of the Scroll in Jerusalem houses the Isaiah manuscripts found in the 1940s. The late dating of Isaiah also violates the consistent witness of history.

No. We must conclude that Isaiah was for real.

So Was Ezekiel

Consider another example.

Both Isaiah and the prophet Ezekiel prophesied the destruction of the powerful commercial center of Tyre. Ezekiel added the intriguing details that the walls and towers of Tyre would be broken, the very dust scraped from her site and that site made like the top of a rock, a place for the spreading of nets (Ezekiel 26:4-5).

At the time of the prediction (588 B.C.) it must have seemed absurd, for Tyre was then indeed a strong city-state. In fact, so well-fortified was the city that for thirteen years (from 585-573 B.C.) it withstood Nebuchadnezzar's attempts to overthrow it. Nebuchadnezzar succeeded only in destroying the mainland fortress, but the island city of Tyre, just a short distance offshore, remained free, and the excellent Phoenician sailors inhabiting it continued their commerce.

But in 332 B.C., Alexander the Great determined to capture

Tyre and constructed a causeway to it. In the process, his army literally scraped the soil from the site of the city down to the bare rock. Mainland Tyre was so devastated that the ancient site can scarcely be identified. Fishermen now spread their nets on the rock where once it stood!

Isaiah, Daniel, Jeremiah, Ezekiel, Micaiah, David, Micah—on and on the list goes of prophets who passed the test. Their prophetic utterances came to pass, for these are historical facts which cannot be successfully disputed.

One more example.

Sir Robert Anderson of Scotland Yard spent many years of his life verifying and validating the details of Daniel's prophecy. Anderson's book, *The Coming Prince*, published in 1890, clearly underscores the fact that the prophet Daniel gave not only specific years but an undeniable sequence for future major events.

Christ's Birth, Life and Death and Resurrection

Concerning the birth, life, death and resurrection of Jesus Christ, over sixty prophetic utterances by more than a dozen different prophets were literally fulfilled—though given, in some cases, as much as 1,000 years prior to His birth.

Peter Stoner, in *Science Speaks*, deals extensively with the science of probability in his examination of biblical prophecy. He refers to just eight of the sixty specific prophecies about the first coming of Christ and says, "We find that the chance that any man might have lived down to the present time and fulfilled all of these eight prophecies is one in 100,000,000,000,000,000."

In order to help us comprehend this staggering probability, Stoner illustrates it by supposing that we mark a silver dollar and then take it and the rest of the 100,000,000,000,000,000 silver dollars and lay them evenly all over the state of Texas. They will cover the entire state to a depth of two feet. Blindfold a man and tell him that he can travel as far as he wishes, but he must pick up only one silver dollar—the marked one.

What chance will he have of selecting the right one? The same chance that the prophets had of writing these eight prophecies and having them all come to pass in any one man—from their day down to the present time. Unless, of course, they did not write them in their own wisdom.

The choice is clear.

Either these prophecies were given by the inspiration of God or the prophets just wrote them as they thought they should be. In the latter case, the prophets had just one chance of having their predictions come true in 100,000,000,000,000,000.

But they all came to pass in Christ.

The fulfillment of these eight prophecies alone affirms that God inspired the words of the prophets to a definiteness that is incomprehensible.

Stoner then considers forty-eight prophecies and says, "We find the chance that any one man fulfilled all 48 prophecies to be 1 in 10 to the 157th power." (That's a one followed by 157 zeroes. We won't waste the space required to include that!) To visualize a number that large is a virtual impossibility.

Remember, however, that it was not just eight or forty-eight, but sixty prophecies that Jesus completely and totally fulfilled. This demonstrates conclusively that prophecies completed in Jesus Christ are a powerful testimony to both His and the prophets' authenticity.

They Were Bona Fide

Obviously, Isaiah, Ezekiel, Daniel and their kin were not mere seers with a record of error or partial accuracy such as modern-day tabloid psychics exhibit. They were prophets whose utterances have been vindicated as being from God. All their prophecies, whose time for fulfillment has arrived, have come to pass with 100-percent accuracy.

Their noble ranks include even Jesus Christ (the greatest of all prophets) and the apostles, like Peter, Paul and John of Patmos, whose Revelation is the final book of the sacred canon.

The word of these men, in terms of prophecies still to be fulfilled, may be completely trusted. Their utterances have the stamp of divine authenticity upon them. While much of what they said is still future, it is apparent that we are beginning to see the fulfillment of many of their predictions in our time.

Note

1 There is one instance in Scripture of false prophets making accurate predictions (Deuteronomy 13:1-5). God apparently permitted this as a test of Israel's loyalty to Him. In such an instance—wherein a false (but accurate) prophet uses his accompishment to lead people into action contrary to the revealed will and word of the Lord—the test of the prophet's authenticity becomes his character and the course of action he is suggesting. Obviously the accurate false prophet is exceedingly dangerous, just as the most dangerous counterfeit is the one most nearly perfect.

Source: William R. Goetz, *Apocalypse Next* (Camp Hill, PA: Horizon Books, 1997), pp. 43-51.

APPENDIX B

Practical Preparations for Potential Y2K Problems

The widespread and growing discussion about the possible effects of Y2K has caused many people to seriously ask what sort of practical preparations they should be making to minimize its potential impact on them and their family.

A wide variety of responses can be found to such a question—ranging all the way from the very basic minimum to very detailed preparations, with some lists running into dozens of items.

As I have researched the various suggestions, it has become apparent that the kinds of vital preparations that can be made by the average citizen fall into four main areas:

1. Security of important documents

2. Provision of food and water; waste disposal

3. Alternative energy sources

4. Source of cash

Quite obviously these are not the only areas of possible

preparation. Proper preparation by businesses is of a much different sort.

As well, several of the four basic areas I've indicated could entail within them a large range of preparations. Consider some of these:

1. Security of Important Documents

At the very minimum, advises Larry Burkett of Christian Financial Concepts, have hard copy records of your taxes, savings, investments, Social Security benefits and banking transactions. Michael Hyatt adds things like proof of age, citizenship, marital status, property owned, mortgages, debts owed and paid and so on. Grant Jeffrey suggests obtaining a written response from your bank verifying their Y2K compliance and switching to a bank that is compliant if yours will not offer a guarantee.

2. Provision of Food and Water; Waste Disposal

The wisdom of stockpiling a supply of food is apparent. If there is no problem, it can be used anyway. A regular pattern of purchasing a few extra nonperishable food items on each trip to the supermarket would make this possible with a minimum of financial hardship.

Water is even more vital than food in the short run. The storage of a water supply in two-liter plastic bottles is wise. Several drops of Clorox makes possible long-term storage of water. It's also sensible to know how to purify water from other sources should such become necessary.

Waste disposal is a delicate subject, but an essential one, should Y2K disruptions be extensive or lengthy. Unless a game plan is in place to deal with the disposal of garbage and human waste, there is a genuinely serious potential for disease. This contingency needs to be faced should municipal sewage and garbage disposal systems not be functional.

3. Alternative Energy Sources

This is crucial, particularly in northern areas, since Y2K will occur in the dead of winter. Seeking guarantees of millennium compliance from your provider is a wise course of action.

The options, as a back-up provision, are fairly straightforward. Gasoline or diesel generators, air-tight stoves, fireplaces, solar heat capability or a combination of these are the basic alternatives to electric and gas supply.

Light can be provided by candles, flashlights, lanterns or lightsticks.

4. Source of Cash

Reports of the actions planned in this regard vary widely from having enough cash to meet needs for a few days to having thousands on hand where possible.

Each person needs to determine on the basis of his or her ability, need and level of concern what course of action to take.

Unquestionably, there is wisdom in having on hand some hedge against disruptions in the banking system or social service payments.

Putting away even a small amount each month will be a help. If there is no crisis, it's money in hand!

A great many other matters could be considered. One author has compiled a baker's dozen—thirteen essential, specific and practical preparations and plans. Another list contains nineteen. A move to a small community, if such is feasible, is advised by some. Contacting your utility providers to be assured of their Y2K compliance is a wise move. Several web sites contain extensive recommendations. Books on the subject are available at most libraries.

The important thing is to determine for yourself what action you will take. Then, as early as possible, follow through on your plan. (The earlier the better, since it is possible that supplies may be limited as the date approaches.)

And simply because you may not be able to do everything you feel you should, don't fail to do what you can. Numerous experts reiterate—any preparation is better than none.

For more information on Y2K, visit some of the Internet web sites which focus on preparation for the Millennium. Several recommended ones are:

- The Cassandra Project: http://cassandraproject.org/howtoprep.html

- Year 2000 Information Center: http://www.year2000.com

- Christian Financial Concepts: www.cfcministry.org/library/Y2K/index.htm

- Gary North's Y2K Links and Forums: http://www.garynorth.com

- http://www.SurviveY2K.com

The Millennium Meltdown by Grant Jeffrey contains an extensive listing of reliable selected and general resource materials and information (books, magazines, web sites, food and equipment suppliers) to help anyone prepare. It is available at virtually any Christian bookstore, as is Michael Hyatt's *Millennium Bug*, another recommended resource. "What to Do When the Chips Are Down," a cassette series by Chuck Missler and Gordon McDonald, is available from The American Family Institute, 1-800-954-1122, extension 500.

Another highly recommended resource is *Y2K: The Millennium Bug* by Shaunti Christine Feldhahn. Formerly a Federal Reserve Financial analyst, Feldhahn has excellent credentials and provides a wealth of practical, biblical suggestions for getting ready for the potential problems the millennium may bring.

But What If It's a False Alarm?
But what if there really isn't a problem on January 1, 2000?

It may very well be that the disasters gloomily predicted by some simply will not occur.

No problem.

Most of the recommended preparations will involve food or materials which can still be utilized. Very little will have been lost for having prepared.

On the other hand, to fail to prepare and then to discover that there's a major problem could mean serious loss. The writer of Proverbs warns, "A prudent man sees danger and takes refuge, but the simple keep going and suffer for it" (Proverbs 22:3).

It's like that with salvation. Even if the whole message of the Bible turned out to be wrong, the person who has lived as a true Christian will have lost nothing. But if the Bible is true (as there is every reason to believe), the one who has failed to become a Christian will have lost everything—forever.

If you have prayed to receive the Lord Jesus Christ as Savior during the reading of *The Economy to Come*, I would be grateful to know of your decision and will be happy to respond with suggestions for growth in your new Christian life.

Kindly address me at:

Dr. Bill Goetz
3825 Hartzdale Drive
Camp Hill, PA 17011